# E... Travel Guide 2013

Published by:

**Bakpak Travelers Guide, Inc.**
PO BOX 10954
Marina del Rey, CA 90295
Phone/Fax: (718) 504-5099
email: info@bakpakguide.com
www.bakpakguide.com

**Publisher & Editor**
David Barish

**Travel Research/Editorial**
Rachel Jones
Dominique Channell
Nina Krieger
Neila Deen
Jesse Shapins
Shilo Urban

**Cover Photos**
Lina Tuv, Elena Elisseeva,
Matej Pribelsky

**Advertising Sales**
David Barish

**Photographs**
Sharon Davis, Alexei Nabarro, Tomislav
Stajduhar, Christopher Laas, Ty Rogers, David
Rose, Ritchie White, Gustavo Fadel, Steven
Allan, Hermann Danzmayr, Nihad Eminovic,
Jennifer Trenchard, Barna Rumpf, Charles Silvey,
Alex Brosa, Stan Rippel, Dainis Derics, Bettina
Pressl, Tom De Bruyne, Rachel Jones

To request an advertising media
kit, email us at: sales@bakpakguide.com

Please send listing requests, updates, stories,
or corrections to: updates@bakpakguide.com

**www.bakpakguide.com**

# ▶▶Intro to Europe

Backpacking and independent travel can be one of the most rewarding experiences of your life. Free to wander and explore on your own terms and at your own pace, you will encounter people from all walks of life, take in some of the most stunning scenery imaginable and develop lasting friendships and memories. They will infinitely live in your senses and ultimately change your perception of life and this world.

Europe, rich in cultural diversity and overflowing with natural beauty, is an excellent destination for the free-spirited independent traveler. From quaint fishing villages in Italy to medieval castles in Scotland, you will feel the history of many centuries, taste the decadence and struggles of rising western civilization and genuinely immerse yourself in authentic modern-day European culture.

As you travel, seek out the authentic, not just the trendy: go for a pint or snack in a small quiet pub in the middle of the afternoon; take day trips to towns outside the big cities; buy a picnic lunch from an outdoor market; and take the time to talk to the locals, even speaking a few words in their language. And, above and beyond all else, respect your host country. Be aware and appreciate your surroundings and you will not only deepen your cultural experience, but defy any loud and intrusive stereotype often attached to tourists.

We at Bakpak Travelers Guides are committed to providing you with informative and helpful information so that you can have a memorable, yet affordable experience. Our lists and summaries are intended for use as a brief outline to your trip. In short, we are not a guide book that provides you with the entire history of each city, nor do we list every conceivable attraction or accommodation. Exploring each city yourself and making last minute decisions based on mood, budget or logistics is part of the backpacking experience.

In this handy, inexpensive guide we tell you the basics, such as a brief summary of each city (i.e.: why you'd want/not want to go there), money, transportation, budget and hostel accommodations and main and/or sleeper attractions. You define and reveal the essence of your trip yourself - whether by talking to locals or other travelers, exploring a sudden discovery or just letting fate, chance or luck (sometimes bad luck) pave the way – your experience will be unique and delightful. **Happy travels!**

## ▸▸Visitor Info

**General Europe**
www.visiteurope.com

**Austria**
www.austria.info/us

**Belgium**
www.visitbelgium.com

**Czech Republic**
www.czechtourism.com

**Denmark**
www.visitdenmark.us

**Finland**
www.visitfinland.com

**France**
www.franceguide.com

**Germany**
www.germany.travel

**Great Britain**
www.visitbritain.com

**Greece**
www.visitgreece.gr

**Hungary**
www.visit-hungary.com

**Ireland**
www.discoverireland.com

**Italy**
www.italia.it/en/home.html

**Luxembourg**
www.ont.lu

**Monaco**
www.visitmonaco.com

**Netherlands**
www.holland.com

**Northern Ireland**
www.ni-tourism.com

**Norway**
www.visitnorway.com

**Scotland**
www.visitscotland.com

**Spain**
www.spain.info

**Sweden**
www.visitsweden.com

**Switzerland**
www.switzerlandtourism.com

**Wales**
www.visitwales.co.uk

**Turkey**
www.goturkey.com

## »Prices/Listings in the Guide

We've tried to be as accurate and up to date as possible, BUT prices may change, places go out of business and the inevitable tide of trendiness may have turned and certain hot spots or suggestions may not be so hot anymore. Be sure to ask the cost before booking or paying for anything. Also, as suggested throughout our guide, pick up the local publication in each city which gives you the most-up-to-date happenings and hip spots to check out.

## »Free Things to See & Do

Throughout the Guide, we have included a Ⓕ symbol next to those attractions, museums, markets and other activities are free. Some are free on certain days of the month, some are free all the time. The goal was to save you money on your trip in as many ways as possible.

## »Money Saving Tips

There are a ton of convenient and practical ways in which to save money without scrimping on your actual experience and enjoyment.

In addition to free things to see and do, look out for the Ⓢ symbol throughout the Guide which denotes an opportunity to save money. You can also try the following tips.

Overnight Train when traveling long distances, take the overnight train to save money on a night's lodging.

Public Transport purchase a public transport 10 pack/day/week pass so you can see as much as possible for as little as possible.

Tourist Info make your first stop the local tourist info center to check for cheap deals, discounts, freebies, goings on and free maps of the city.

Local Markets shop in the local markets for a cheap picnic of fresh local delicacies. Hit the market and take advantage of your hostel's kitchen facilities.

## »Keep In Touch With Us!

Some of the most valuable information and correspondence we get is directly from our readers. If you've discovered the best lodging, café or bar, send us an e-mail. If something we suggested is completely off the radar (un-cool or closed) definitely let us know. Or, if you just have general comments or suggestions about our guide (good or bad), we and other travelers would love to know, so drop us a line any time using the following email addresses: **Listing/Content Updates -** *updates@bakpakguide.com.* **Suggestions of places to add, stories, etc** *content@bakpakguide.com.*

## »Safety Tips

Many large European cities are known for their high incidence of pickpocketing and thievery. Travel smart: be on guard, yet be reasonable. Be curious, but trust your instincts. Here are a few tips.

Valuables keep your money and valuable documents (passport, airline/rail tickets) close to your body – preferably in a money belt that is strapped under your clothing next to your body.

Copies of Documents keep a copy of your valuable documents (passport, tickets) and credit card emergency numbers in a separate place from the originals and leave a set of copies at home. Some websites offer secure document storage for little or no charge.

Pickpockets don't get caught in large crowds (3 or more) where pickpockets can easily overwhelm you.

Luggage keep your luggage within eyeshot, or if you plan on sleeping on the train, fasten it to the rack with a padlock.

Day Pack if you have a day pack, keep it at the front of your body so that it cannot be zipped open without you knowing. Use small locks for extra safety to avoid the petty thieves.

## »Notes

_____

_____

_____

_____

_____

_____

_____

_____

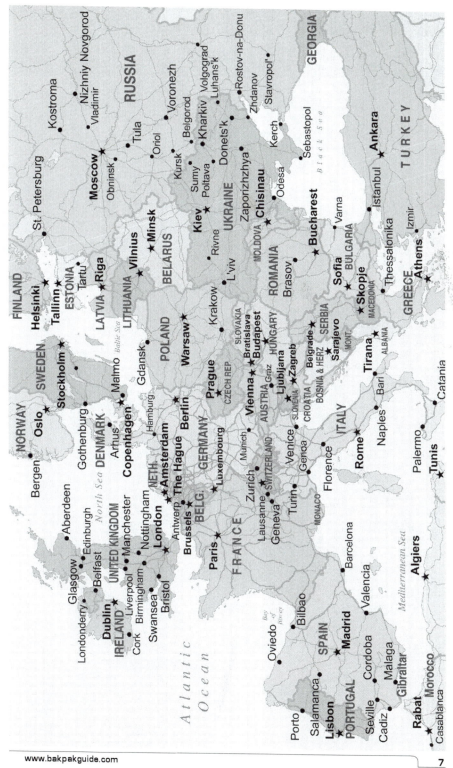

# ▸▸Getting Around

Oslo

Stockholm

*(330mi/530km/ 6.75hrs)*

*(365mi/590km/ .75hrs)*

**Copenhagen**

*(50mi/80km/ 1hr)*

Glasgow  •Edinburgh

*(105mi/170km)*

*(90mi/145km/ 2.25hrs)*  •Belfast

**Dublin**

*(395mi/635km/ 6.5hrs)*

**Amsterdam**

*(380mi/610km/ 5.5hrs)*  ★ **Berlin**

*(310mi/500km/ 5.5hrs via chun.)*

*(130mi/210km/ 2.25hrs)*

*(200mi/325km/ 4.5hrs)*

*(350mi/565km/ 9.5hrs via Ferry)*

**London**  ★

Cologne

*(310mi/500km/ 4.5hrs)*

**Brussels** ★

**Prague**

*(265mi/425km/ 4.5hrs)*

Frankfurt

*(310mi/500km/5hrs)*

*(175mi/280km/ 3.5hrs)*

*(185mi/ 300km/3hrs)*

*(235mi/380km/ 3.5hrs)*

**Vienna**

**Paris**

*(245mi/400km /3.75hrs)*  •Munchen

*(145mi/235km/2.25hrs)*

★

**Budapest**

Brussels-Cologne *(125mi/205km/2.25hrs)*

*(405mi/650km/ 6.5hrs))*

*(190mi/305km/ 3.25hrs)*

Zurich

Frankfurt-Cologne *(110mi/175km/1.5hrs)*

*(350mi/570km/ 6.25hrs)*

*(390mi/630km/ 6hrs)*

*(675mi/1085km/ 10.5hrs)*

*(580mi/935km/ 9hrs)*

Nice

*(255mi/410km/ 4hrs)*

Firenze

*(140mi/230km/ 2.25hrs)*

*(365mi/590km/ 6hrs)*

*(390mi/630km/ 6hrs)*

★ **Rome**

Barcelona

**Madrid**★

*(375mi/605km/ 5.75hrs)*

★

**Lisbon**

## ⏩Airfare around Europe

Once you arrive, there are more deals now for flying around Europe than ever before! Options include airpasses, flight coupons and discount airlines.

### ⏩Air Pass
**Europe by Air**
They offer flight coupons for $69 or $129 to many destinations in Europe on various European airlines. You can purchase as many coupons as you like and can open-date your tickets as well. www.europebyair.com

### ⏩Discount Airlines
Over the last few years, a number of new, smaller airlines have surfaced offering incredibly low prices for regional European flights. These airlines use regional and alternative city airports so convenience might be sacrificed for price, although these airports are now becoming more integral to inter-Europe travel. If you are short on time, these rates can be cheaper than rail travel and, more importantly, time saving!

**Ryan Air**
They operate hubs out of London, Dublin and Glasgow to many destinations in mainland Europe. Rates at the time of publication were as low as £18 round trip from London to Dublin (we didn't forget a zero). Prices generally run in the £20-£90 price range r/t. Be warned, though, that delays and strandings overnight at airports do occur. www.ryanair.com

**easyJet**
They fly over 28 routes to 18 key cities using hubs in London Stansted and Liverpool, England and Geneva, Switzerland. Prices range from £30 to £90+ round trip. www.easyjet.com

**Brussels Airlines/Virgin-Express**
From their hub in Brussels they fly to London, Rome, Barcelona, Berlin, Copenhagen, Madrid and many more European cities starting at €58 one-way. Also fly worldwide. www.brusselsairlines.com

**Air Berlin**
Out of Berlin-Tegel, this airline flies across Europe to many major city destinations from €40 including all taxes and fuel surcharges. www.airberlin.com

## ⏩Coach Travel

**Busabout**
Offers a hop-on, hop-off backpacker coach network (70 destinations) around Europe. While on the bus it's a tour and the guides will book your accommodation and activities for you as you travel around. You

## ⏩Notes

can travel on their Flexitrip Pass, creating your own route and places to stop. Or you can choose from one of three "loop" routes (Northern, Southern or Western). The Flexitrip Pass costs $595 with 6 Flexistops, $50 for each additional Flexistop. Loop Passes cost from $685-$1429 for adults, $659-$1375 for students. www.busabout.com

### Eurolines
Offers point to point tickets or passes for travel throughout 46 cities. Depending upon the travel season, unlimited travel passes cost: 15 days - €210-€350/adults, €180-$295/youth, 30 days - €315-$460/ adults, €245-$380/youth. www.eurolines.com

## ▸▸Point to Point Rail Travel

### ▸▸Point to Point Rail
A number of rail companies offer point to point rail schedules and ticket purchase online with a credit card. Tickets can be mailed or picked up at the departing station.

### Eurostar
Using sleek high-speed trains, Eurostar can take you from the center of London to Brussels or Paris in only 3 hours. Fares start at £63. www.eurostar.com

### Thalys
High-speed trains (Paris to Brussels in 1.5hrs) connecting Paris, Amsterdam and Koln via Brussels and from Paris to Geneva with many stops in between. Weekday, return Mini tickets are the cheapest fares. www.thalys.com

## ▸ Backpacker Tours & Transport

There are a number of tours and backpacker-geared transport for countrywide and regional European travel that include hostels or budget hotels. **Prices are in US dollars unless otherwise noted.**

### ▸▸Hop-on, Hop-off Transport
The popular **hop-on, hop-off** tours allow you to travel the route at your own pace over a given amount of time. While on the bus, it's like a tour, but you can get off any time and catch the next bus coming through.

### Busabout (Europe wide)
Offers a hop-on, hop-off backpacker coach network (70 destinations) around Europe. While on the bus it's a tour and the guides will book your accommodation and activities for you as you travel around. You can travel on their Flexitrip Pass, creating your own route and places to stop. Or you can choose from one of three "loop" routes (Northern, Southern or Western). The Flexitrip

## ▸▸Featured Operators
### EUROLINES
*Eurolines offers you the freedom of Europe with the Eurolines Pass. Get unlimited travel around Europe for 15 or 30 days. The pass offers total flexibility with the choice of planning your route in advance or booking as you travel - all for one excellent value price.*
www.eurolines.com

## ▸▸National Rail Links
**Belgian Railway**
www.b-rail.be

**Deutche Bahn (Germany)**
www.bahn.de

**Netherlands Railway**
www.ns.nl

**Eurostar**
www.eurostar.com

**Scotrail**
www.firstscotrail.com

**Iamród Éireann (Ireland)**
www.irishrail.ie

**Virgin Trains (UK)**
www.virgintrains.co.uk

**RENFE (Spain)**
www.renfe.es

**SNCF (France)**
www.sncf.com

**Trenitalia (Italy)**
www.trenitalia.com

**Swiss Federal Railways**
www.sbb.ch

**ÖBB (Austria)**
www.oebb.at

Pass costs $595 with 6 Flexistops, $50 for each additional Flexistop. Loop Passes cost from $685-$1429 for adults, $659-$1375 for students. www.busabout.com

## ⟩Backpacker Tours (7+ days)
### Travel Talk Tours (Turkey & Greece)
Offers adventure tours of Turkey, 8-12 days, costing £419-879+ and 8-10 day Greek Island tours for £499-779. www.traveltalktours.com

### Fez Travel (Turkey & Greece)
Fez Travel offers tours around Turkey and Greece including the 10 day Magic Carpet tour ($895-1159) or the 12 day Orient Express ($1,439). Both include hotel, meals and transport but exclude kitty payment.

They also offer budget Fez Bus Tours around Western Turkey including their 14-day Turkish Delight Tour ($869US). The 6-day Aegean Trail Tour costs $499US. www.feztravel.com

## ⟩Backpacker Tours (2 to 7 days)
### Haggis Adventures (England/Wales)
The 5-day Cornwall Crusader covers the hot spots of England while their 5-day Welsh Explorer takes you through Wales and its countryside. Both tours depart from and return to London and cost $339-359. Tours include transport and driver but exclude food. www.haggisadventures.com

### Haggis Adventures (Scotland)
Haggis offers 2 to 10 day tours of Scotland from $129 including the popular 3-day Skye High ($205), a 5-day Highland Fling ($329), a 7-day Island Explorer ($489-575) and a 10-day Compass Buster tour ($699-739). Tours include transport and driver but exclude food. www.haggisadventures.com

### MacBackpackers (Scotland)
Offers a variety of 1, 3 & 5 day tours including The Isle of Skye, Loch Ness, glens, castles and battlefields (costs from £69 to £305). All tours depart from and return to Edinburgh. www.macbackpackers.com

### Paddywagon (Ireland)
Offers 2-4, 6 and 10 day tours from Dublin to Northern and southern Ireland and all Ireland ranging from $192-$654. Tours include accommodation, breakfast and entry fees. www.paddywagontours.com

### Shamrocker Tours (Ireland)
See the south, west or northern regions of Ireland on their popular 3-day ($209-219), 5-day ($359-379) and 7-day ($529-565) tours from departing and returning to Dublin. Tours include transport and driver. www.shamrockeradventures.com

⟩Notes

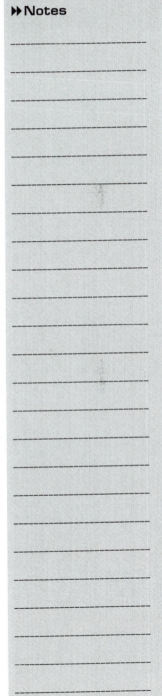

# ▶▶UK & Ireland

Shetland Islands
Lerwick

Orkney Islands

Hebrides

Inverness

**SCOTLAND**

Glasgow
Edinburgh

Sunderland

Londonderry
**NORTHERN IRELAND**
Belfast

U. K.

Leeds

Galway   **IRELAND**
**Dublin**
Liverpool   Manchester

Limerick
Birmingham   Leicester

Cork   Waterford   **WALES**

Swansea   **ENGLAND**

Bristol   **London**

Dover

*English Channel*

Plymouth

## ⏵England

### ⏵London

See **page 18** for complete London Information.

### ⏵Southern England

This region of England offers a variety of historical and adventure activities, beautiful landscapes, coasts and cultural sites. Popular stops include:

**Brighton**, known as Little London by the sea; **Bath**, a National Heritage City discovered by the Romans; and **Bristol**, located at the heart of the South West, which is a great base from which to explore the region.

The **Devon** area has a few university towns, including **Exeter**, and offers excellent seaside resorts, walking opportunities, historical sites and dolphin spotting. Other towns in this region include **Exmoor**, **Dartmoor**, **Plymouth** and **Torquay**.

The **Cornwall** region is an excellent place to enjoy the rugged coast and hang ten on the surfboard. Walking opportunities also abound. Towns to visit include **Newquay** and **St. Ives** (surfing spots) as well as **Penzance**, **Sennen** and **Zennor**. Don't miss stopping at **Land's End**, the very tip of England and the must-see **Stonehenge**, located 2 miles outside of Amesbury in Wiltshire.

### ⏵Heart of England

The center region of England offers a variety of cultural and historic sites ranging from cities like **Manchester** and **Liverpool** to fabled shires such as **Nottingham**. And don't forget the birthplace of Shakespeare in **Stratford-upon-Avon** or the **Cotswold** region in Gloucestershire.

### ⏵Northern England

The north of England offers many excellent stops on your way to Scotland including the university town of **Newcastle-upon-Tyne**, the town of **York** and the **Yorkshire Moores**, the **Lakes District** and **Isle of Mann** on the west coast.

The **Lakes District** sits just under the Scottish border in Cumbria County. This breathtaking region envelops you with its magnificent lakes, mountains and valleys. If you're Scotland bound, it's a terrific and peaceful stop where you can go hiking, climbing or just unwind.

## ⏵Scotland

Indeed one of the most picturesque countries you'll ever visit, it is by no means an extension of England. Scotland is known for its beautiful highlands, castles, clans and offers a variety of outdoor activities including rock climbing, white water rafting and even snowboarding in the winter. The **Highlands** are a must see, as are the many lochs, castles and former battle-

## ⏵Visitor Info

**Great Britain** www.visitbritain.com

**Ireland** www.tourismireland.com

**Northern Ireland** www.ni-tourism.com

**Scotland** www.visitscotland.com

**Wales** www.visitwales.com

## ⏵Quick Facts

**Calling Information**

*Country Codes*: 44 UK, 353 Ireland

*Calling in the UK/Ireland*: add a "0" before the area code

*Calling overseas*: 00+country code+area code+number

**Currency & Exchange Rates**

*Currency*: British Pound (£) - England, Wales, Scotland and N. Ireland; Euro (€) Ireland.

*Currency Breakdown*: 100 Pence equals £1; 100 cents=1 €

*Exchange Rates*: £1 costs: US$1.61/ €1.24/ AUD$1.53/CAN$1.59

*Exchange Rates*: €1 costs: US$1.30/ £.81/AUD$1.24/ CAN$1.28

field sites that adorn Scotland's countryside. Don't miss Inverness, Fort William, Loch Ness, Aberdeen, the Isle of Skye, and Eilean Donan Castle. There are a host of great tour companies that can get you around Scotland without making a dent in your budget.

## ➤➤Inverness

Inverness is the capital of the Highlands and most famous for the legends of the **Loch Ness Monster** and the lesser known **Big Lassy** (you'll find out boys). There is tons on offer here including stunning scenery, lots of lochs and glens, castles and the **Culloden Battlefield**.

## ➤➤Isle of Skye

A trip to the Isle of Skye is highly recommended. Plan on staying at least 2 nights so you can catch the excellent day tour available around 11am-noon, daily. Most hostels are located in **Kyleakin** and only a few minutes' walk from the ferry drop off. By day you can rent a bike, hike, take a nature boat tour or explore other parts of the Island. At night, join or start a pub crawl - there are only 2 or 3 pubs, all within a stone's throw of each other.

## ➤➤Oban

Oban is a quaint seaside town on the West Coast of Scotland, north of Glasgow and south of Fort William. It is a good place to stop on your way back to Edinburgh or Glasgow from the Highlands. On offer are boat trips, ferries to nearby Islands including **Mull**, and the **Oban Distillery**.

## ➤➤Northern Ireland

A trip to Northern Ireland is highly recommended. It may just well make your visit to take the day tour to **Belfast**. It includes an unbelievable ride in a black taxi through the Catholic and Protestant sections of Belfast as well as a walking tour through the Catholic section. Two to six day tours are also available to Northern Ireland that stop in Belfast, Omagh and Londonderry.

## ➤➤Republic of Ireland

Ireland's countryside is as beautiful as it gets and no trip to Ireland should be made without venturing out of Dublin. Attractions to visit include Blarney Castle, the Cliffs of Moher, and the Rock of Cashel. Places to visit include Cork, Dingle, Killarney, Galway and Killkenney.

## ➤➤Cork (Southwest)

Cork is the largest county in Ireland, with everything to offer from lively **Cork City** with its charming footbridges, to the village of **Blarney** known for its famous castle, to the town of **Ballycotton** with an expansive port and rugged cliff views. Cork offers

golden beaches, beautiful rolling green hills and a vibrant culture in its main city. **To See/Do**: Blarney Castle, Cobh (Great Island), Cork City, Ballyhoura Mountain Park and Millstreet.

### ▶▶Kerry (Southwest)

One of the most picturesque parts of Ireland, county Kerry is just breathtaking. Drive through rural sheep-dotted landscapes and endless mountains amidst unexpected wildlife, majestic lakes and imposing coastline views. The towns and villages of **Killarney**, **Kenmare** and **Dingle**, just to name a few, are welcoming, friendly and offer an authentic taste of small-town Ireland. You can see most of the "must-see" destinations on the Ring of Kerry Drive along N70/71. **To See/Do**: Dingle, Ring of Kerry coastline/Iveragh Peninsula, Killarney National Park and Ladies View.

### ▶▶Clare (West)

Perched on the west coast between the raw genuine beauty of Galway and the idyllic landscape of county Kerry lies charming County Clare. Among miniature colorful villages is such gorgeous scenery as the renowned **Cliffs of Moher** and the unique limestone caverns of the **Burren** region. We recommend staying in either Galway or County Kerry and then taking a scenic day trip.

### ▶▶Galway (West)

A juxtaposition of the rough, untrampled natural beauty of Connemara mountain and the bustling thriving energy of the city of Galway makes this an essential stop on any tour of Ireland. Located on the island's west coast, county Galway is where old Gaelic Ireland retains its distinct and genuine character. You will encounter some of the friendliest locals whether you're driving through wild bog landscape amidst a tiny village of thatched roof houses or having your fourth pint with a University student in town...it's the best of both worlds. For an ideal stay, make your base the city itself. **To See/Do**: Aran Islands, Connemara Mountain and National Park, Galway City and Clifden.

### ▶▶Donegal (North)

As you go northwest in Ireland, Gaelic beauty and culture becomes even more dramatic. The rough coastline of Donegal hosts spectacular wildlife, beaches, and fishing ports, and is infused with centuries of history and folklore. Drive through the villages and towns of the **Gaeltacht** (Gaelic) region to appreciate this area's authenticity. **To See/Do**: Deeryveagh Mountains, Glenveagh Castle & National Park and Ring Fort.

▶▶**Notes**

## ▶England

### ▶London

See page 19-22 for Featured Hostels in London.

### ▶Southern England

**Bath Backpackers Hostel**
12 Pierrepoint Street, *Bath*
(01225-446-787)

**City of Bath YMCA**
Int'l House. Broad St. Place, *Bath*
(01225-325-900)

**St. Christophers Inn**
9 Green Street, *Bath*
(122-548-1444)
*See their Featured Hostel Listing on page 14*

**Baggies Backpackers**
33 Oriental Place, *Brighton*
(01273-733-740)

**Journeys Brighton Hostel**
33 Richmond Place, *Brighton*
(01273-695-866)

**St. Christophers Inn**
10-12 Grand Junction Rd, *Brighton*
(127-320-2035)
*See their Featured Hostel Listing on page 14*

**Bristol Backpackers**
17 St. Stephens Street, *Bristol*
(01179-257-900)

**Bristol YHA**
14 Narrow Quay, *Bristol*
(01179-221-659)

**Globe Backpackers**
71 Holloway St., *Exeter*
(01392-215-521)

**Glastonbury Backpackers**
The Crown, 4 Market Pl, *Glastonbury*
(01458-833-353)

**Ocean Backpackers**
29 St. James Place, *Ilfracombe*
(01271-867-835)

**Newquay Backpackers**
69-73 Tower Road, *Newquay*
(01637-879-366)

**St. Christophers Inn**
35 Fore Street, *Newquay*
(163-785-9111)
*See their Featured Hostel Listing on page 14*

**Plymouth Backpackers**
172 Citadel Road, The Hoe,
*Plymouth* (01752-225-158)

**Portsmouth Foyer**
22 Edinburgh Rd, *Portsmouth*
(02392-360-001)

**Portsmouth & Southsea Backpackers**
4 Florence Road, *Southsea*
(02392-832-495)

**St. Ives Backpackers**
Town Center, *St. Ives*
(01736-799-444)

**Torquay Backpackers**
119 Abbey Road, *Torquay*
(01803-299-924)

### ▶Heart of England

**Hatters Hostel**
92–95 Livery Street, *Birmingham*
(0121-236-4031)

**Embassie Indep. Hostel**
1 Falkner Square, *Liverpool*
(0151-707-1089)

**Hatters Hostel**
56-60 Mount Pleasant, *Liverpool*
(0151-709-5570)

**International Inn**
4 South Hunter St., *Liverpool*
(0151-709-8135)

**Hatters Hostel**
50 Newton Street, *Manchester*
(0161-236-9500)

**Manchester Backpackers**
41-43 Great Stone Rd, Stretford,
*Manchester.* (0161-872-3499)

**Woodies Backpackers**
19 Blossom St, Ancoats,
*Manchester.* (0161-228-3456)

**Igloo Backpackers Hostel**
110 Mansfield Rd, *Nottingham*
(01159-475-250)

**Oxford Backpackers**
9a Hythe Bridge Road, *Oxford*
(01865-721-761)

**Stratford-Upon-Avon Backpackers**
33 Greenhill Street
(01789-263-838)

### ▶Northern England

**York Backpackers Hostel**
88 Micklegate, *York*
(01904-627-720)

**York Youth Hotel**
11-13 Bishophill Senior, *York*
(01904-625-904)

## ▶Wales

**Cardiff Backpackers Hostel**
98 Neville Street , *Cardiff*
(029-20-345-577)

**Hamilton Backpackers**
21-23 Hamilton St., Fishguard,
*Pembrokshire* (01348-874-797)

**Totter's Backpackers**
2 High Street, *Caernarfon*
(01286-672-963)

**Stonecroft Hostel**
Stonecroft House, Dolecoed Rd.
*Llanwrtyd Wells* (01591-610-327)

## ▶Scotland

### ▶Edinburgh

See page 24 for Featured Hostels in Edinburgh.

### ▶Glasgow

See page 25 for hostels in Glasgow.

### ▶Inverness

**Bazpackers Hostel**
Culduthel Road
(01463-717-663)

**Eastgate Backpackers Hostel**
38 Eastgate
(01463-718-756)

**Inverness Youth Hostel**
Victoria Drive
(01463-231-771

**Inverness Student Hotel**
8 Culduthel Road
(01463-236-556)

### ▶Isle of Skye

**Skye Backpackers**
Kyleakin.
(01599-534-510)

**Saucy Mary's**
Kyleakin.
(01599-534-845)

**Dun Flodigary Hostel**
Flodigary By Straffin
(01470-552-212)

**Skyewalker Hostel**
Portnalong.
(01478-640-250)

### ▶Oban

**Oban Backpackers**
Breadalbane Street
(01631-562-107)

**Oban Youth Hostel**
Esplanade.
(01631-562-025)

## ▸Other Scotland Hostels

**Loch Ness Backpackers**
Coiltie Farmhouse,
East Lewiston *Drumnadrochit.*
(01456-450-807)

**Morag's Lodge**
Bunnoch Brae, *Fort Augustus*
(01320-368-289)

**Ft. William Backpackers**
Alma Road, *Fort William*
(01397-700-711)

**Braincroft Bunkhouse**
Braincroft, Crieff, *Perthshire*
(01764-670140)

**St. Andrews Tourist Hostel**
Inchape House, St. Marys Place,
(01334-479-911)

**Willy Wallace Hostel**
77 Murray Pl., *Stirling*
(01786-446-773)

## ▸Northern Ireland

**Armagh Hostel**
9 Abbey Street, *Armagh*
(028-3751-1800)

**Arnie's Backpacker's**
63 Fitzwilliam Street, *Belfast*
(01232-242-867)

**Belfast International Youth Hostel**
22-32 Donegall Road, *Belfast*
(028-9031-5435)

**Linen House Hostel**
18 Kent Street, *Belfast*
(01232-586-400)

**Vagabonds Belfast**
9 University Road, *Belfast*
(028-9023-3017)

**Omagh Indep. Hostel**
Glenhordial 9a Waterworks Rd,
*Omagh* (01662-241-973)

## ▸Ireland

### ▸Dublin

See page 26 for Featured Hostels in Dublin.

See page 26 for Featured Hostels in Dublin.

### ▸Wicklow (Southeast)

**Avonmore House**
Ferrybank Arklow
(0402-3285)

**Wicklow Bay Hostel**
Marine House
(0404-69213)

## ▸Cork (Southwest)

**Aaron House**
Lower Glanmire Road
(021-4551-566)

**Isaac's Hostel**
48 MacCurtain Street
(021-4508-388)

**Kinlay House Shandon**
Bob & Joan Walk, *Shandon*
(021-4508-966)

**Sheila's Hostel**
4 Belgrave Place, Wellington Rd
(021-4505-562)

## ▸Kerry (Southwest)

**Sive Hostel**
East End, *Cahersiveen*
(066-947-2717)

**Bog View Hostel**
*Lougher Annascaul*
(066-915-8125)

**Ballintaggart House**
Racecourse Rd., *Dingle*
(066-915-1454)

**Grapevine Hostel**
Dykegate St., *Dingle*
(066-915-2434)

**Rainbow Hostel**
Dingle Town, *Dingle*
(066-915-1044)

**Failte Hostel**
Shelbourne St., *Kenmare*
(064-42333)

**Killarney Railway Hostel**
Killarney Town Centre, *Killarney*
(064-35299)

**Neptune's Town Hostel**
New Street, *Killarney*
(064-35255)

**Paddy's Palace Killarney**
31 New Street, *Killarney*
(064-35382)

**Westward Court**
Mary Street, *Tralee*
(066-718-0081)

### ▸Clare (West)

**Aille River Hostel**
*Doolin* (065-707-4260)

**Paddy's Doolin Hostel**
Fisher Street, *Doolin*
(065-707-4006)

**The Clare Hostel**
Summerhill, *Ennis*
(065-682-9370)

**Katie O'Connors**
Frances Street, *Kilrush*
(065-905-1133)

**Lahinch Hostel**
Church Street, *Lahinch*
(065-708-1040)

**Liscannor Village Hostel**
*Liscannor.*
(065-708-1550)

## ▸Galway (West)

**Barnacle's Quay Street**
10 Quay Street, *Galway City*
(091-568-644)

**Great Western House**
Frenchville Lane,
Eyre Square, *Galway City.*
(091-561-139)

**Kinlay House Eyre Square**
Merchants Road,
Eyre Square, *Galway City*
(091-565-244)

**Salmon Weir Hostel**
Woodquay, *Galway City*
(091-561-133)

**SleepZone**
Bothar na mBan, *Woodquay,*
*Galway* (91-566-999)

**Woodquay Hostel**
23-24 Woodquay, *Galway City*
(091-562-618)

## ▸Donegal (North)

**Cliffview Hostel**
Coast Road (N56), *Donegal Town*
(073-216840)

**Malin Head Hostel**
Port Ronanpier, *Malin Head*
Insihowen Co. (077-70289)

# ▶▶London

**LONDON** defies all expectations. This cornerstone of western civilization is hip yet traditional, edgy yet gracious. Whether you're seeking the hippest club or looking for a dose of history and culture, London does not disappoint. Packed with all forms of entertainment, stylish shops, grand monuments, museums and of course, British wit and hospitality, it is an exciting playground for just about everyone.

Go for a ride on a double-decker bus, grab a pint at an old ale house, get your ration of Shepard's pie or beans and eggs. Also make sure you indulge in the numerous international delights and festivities in town. One of the more alluring, and often surprising, facets of London is its rich cultural diversity. England's colonial legacy has today marked its capital as one of the most multicultural cities in Europe. There are tons of ethnic enclaves and neighborhoods brimming with little restaurants and shops serving up some of the most delicious meals and displaying interesting knick-knacks from around the world. Indulge in its cosmopolitan flair and you'll find London at once captivating and inviting, sophisticated and down to earth.

Beware of your cash flow, though. London is far from a budget traveler's dream - it has the second highest cost of living worldwide next to Tokyo. Plan carefully in terms of lodging, meals and traveling around and you'll be treated to an exceptional experience unrivaled by any other city in Europe.

## ▶▶Getting There

See **pages 8-11** for information on tours and transport to and from London and England.

### ▶▶From the Airport

London is generally the most common and cheapest entry-point for visitors to continental Europe. It is served by two international airports, **Heathrow** (LHR) - the busiest in the world - and **Gatwick** (GTW). Both airports lie on the outskirts of the city with easily accessible rail transport into the city of London.

### From Heathrow Airport

The cheapest option to London is the Underground (or "tube"). The **Piccadilly Line** runs from Heathrow terminals to the heart of the city. The fare is £5 one-way. The trip takes about 50-60 minutes and runs frequently until 11:30pm daily. www.tfl.gov.uk

The new **Heathrow Connect** to/from Paddington Station costs £9.10 o/w, £17.80 r/t and take about 25 minutes. www.heathrowconnect.com

## ▶Visitor Info

www.visitlondon.com

See page 96 for London city maps

## ▶▶Quick Facts

**Calling Information**
*Country Code*: 44

*Calling in the UK*: add a "0" before the area code

*Calling overseas*: 00+country code+area code+number

**Currency & Exchange Rates**
*Currency*: British Pound (£)

*Currency Breakdown*: 100 Pence equals £1

*Exchange Rates*: £1 costs: US$1.61/ €1.24/ AUD$1.53/CAN$1.59

**Must See/Must Do**
Fish n' chips, Old London Town, English Countryside

**Say What!**
Subway=Tube; Toilet=Loo; Cigarette=Fag; Kiss=Snog

If you are in a hurry, the **Heathrow Express** train zips non-stop to Paddington station in 15-20 minutes for £18 one-way, £34 round-trip. From there, you can catch a taxi or transfer to the various tube stations. www.heathrowexpress.com

## From Gatwick Airport

The **Gatwick Express** train departs between 4:30am and 1:30am from the airport to Victoria station, London and takes 30-35 minutes. Cost is £18.90 o/w, £33.20 r/t. From there, you can catch a taxi or transfer to the various tube stations. www.gatwickexpress.com

## From Stansted Airport

Many of the low-cost airlines now use this airport as their main hub. The **Stansted Express** train operates 24hrs from the airport to Liverpool St. station in 45 minutes for £22.50 o/w, £31.50 r/t. From there, you can catch a taxi or transfer to the various tube stations. www.stanstedexpress.com

## ⓢ Paddington Station Check-in

On the day of your flight, instead of trekking all your gear to the airport, you can check your bags at the airline check-in desks at Paddington Station (your luggage is sent ahead to the airport). This way you can spend your last hours exploring the city without your luggage and then take either the tube or one of the express trains to the airport.

## ⟫Rail

If you are arriving in London by rail from mainland Europe, it will most likely be via the famed Chunnel. The masterpiece of modern engineering that now links Britain and France is not cheap; however you arrive directly into the beautifully redeveloped **Waterloo** station on the south side of the Thames. Other major rail arrival points include **Victoria** and **Paddington** Stations. Connections to various tube lines are available from all three stations.

## ⟫Bus

Many long-distance bus lines travel to and from London (via train through the Chunnel or ferry). On a single bus you can traverse the entire European continent to Istanbul, Turkey. The major coach company is **National Express** (affiliated with Eurolines). Its buses arrive and depart from **Victoria Coach Station**, adjacent to the Victoria train station.

## ⟫Ferry

A sometimes comfortable and often very affordable means of reaching Britain and London from Europe is by boat. Ferries leave from Germany, Scandinavia, the Netherlands, Belgium, France, Spain and other countries for various British ports, the largest of which is Dover.

## » Getting Around

London's subway system, the **Underground** (the "tube" www.tfl.gov.uk), is probably the most famous in the world. One of the first to be built, the tube today runs as well as any other in the world. It is the best and most efficient way to get around London.

A single fare is based on zones and ranges from £4.30 to £20.20. If you use the Osyter Card and pay as you go, you will pay much less than the cash fare. Or opt for an unlimited **Travelcard** for only £8.40 (zones 1 & 2) which can be used on the tube, buses and light rail after 9:30am daily and all day on the weekends or £8.40 anytime. The **weekly card** is £29.20 (zone 1-2).

Please note that the London tube map is not always geographically correct - some subway stops are very far apart - often not realy walking distance.

Don't forget the infamous double-decker buses. These icons of London are great for sightseeing around town and essential after midnight when the tube stops running. The letter "N" before the number denotes the night buses. Single fares cost £1.35 to £4.20. The Travel Card is valid on these buses.

## » Things to See & Do

### » Tourist Information

The **Britain Visitor Centre** is located near Piccadilly Circus at 1 Regent Street. A large tourist office can also be found in Victoria Station, which offers help with accommodation bookings. Smaller branches are located at Paddington and Waterloo stations and at Gatwick and Heathrow airports.

### » Visitor Discount Cards & Passes

Ⓢ **London Pass**

Pay one price and get free admission/travel card for transport to over 55 attractions, museums, tours, etc. Passes are available for 1 (£46), 2 (£61), 3 (£74) and 6 (£99) days. www.londonpass.com

Ⓢ **English Heritage Overseas Visitor Pass**

Get unlimited free entry to over 100 of England's finest castles, abbeys, Roman remains and prehistoric monuments including the awe-inspiring Stonehenge, Dover Castle and the Secret Wartime Tunnels. Costs only £23 for a 9-day pass, £27 for 16 days. www.english-heritage.org.uk (under Properties).

### » Neighborhoods
**East End**

London's East End is one of the most enjoyable, interesting, and affordable neighborhoods to explore. Once infamous as **Jack the Ripper's** haunt,

## » Featured Hostels

**ST CHRISTOPHER'S INN - THE OASIS**
161-165 Borough High St., *Southwark*
Dorms £10+; T: Hammersmith
(207-407-6266)
www.st-christophers.co.uk/london
*Kick back at this fantastic female only hostel minutes from London Bridge train station. If you can tear yourself away from this great London Hostel then be sure to take a right at the river to marvel at London Bridge.*

**ST CHRISTOPHER'S INN HAMMERSMITH**
28 Hammersmith Bway, *Hammersmith*
Dorms £10+; T: Hammersmith
(208-748-5285)
www.st-christophers.co.uk/london
*Right in the heart of West London's transport hub, this hostel is the ideal location for exploring London. We're right next door to one of London's biggest bus stations. You can't get more central London!*

**ST CHRISTOPHER'S INN CAMDEN**
48-50 Camden High Street, *Camden* Dorms £10+; T: Camden Town station (207 388 1012)
www.st-christophers.co.uk/london
*Be bohemian north of the city centre in this London Backpacker's Hostel. Party with the rock bands at Belushi's, shop around the famous Camden Markets and drink a little Jager into the early hours, at one of the best Hostels in London.*

**ST CHRISTOPHER'S INN GREENWICH**
189 Greenwich High Road, *Greenwich*
Dorms £10+; Train: Greenwich
(208-748-5285)
www.st-christophers.co.uk/london
*Escape the smog but stay within striking distance of the city centre in one of the best London Backpackers Hostels. Launch yourself into Greenwich Park or walk under the river Thames, through an amazing tunnel.*

this historic conglomerate of formerly immigrant neighborhoods is now a lively, ethnically mixed, and young section of the city. It is here that many students and artists come to London and attempt to set up shop.

**Brick Lane** is an excellent East End street to explore. At the southernmost part of Brick Lane near the Aldgate East tube stop and Whitechapel High Street, is a long string of Bangladeshi restaurants and shops. Even the street signs in this area are in Bengali. As you proceed north, exploring off-beat furniture and Bangladeshi outposts, you will find several of the most charming and down-to-earth coffee shops in London.

Also check out the one of the best flower markets in London. On Sunday morning, **Columbia Road** erupts into a fantastic array of beautiful colors. Just don't show up any other time, as this otherwise quaint and attractive street may be completely dead.

## Islington

In recent years Islington has become increasingly popular and youthful. Lining Upper Street between the Angel tube stop and the Highbury and Islington tube stations are some of the most affordable, yet most delicious restaurants in London. You will also find many fantastic, low-key bars in this exciting, authentic London neighborhood. Islington is a great place to spend a night out and get away from the swarms of tourists in SoHo.

## Ⓕ Portobello Market

If you are into antiques, knick-knacks, second hand clothing and the like, head to this market on Saturdays. Located off Kensington Park Road in Notting Hill. Take the tube to Notting Hill Gate.

## Camden Town

London's punk (and tourist scene) at its best! **Camden Town Market** is the center of this constantly bustling area. Here, not only will you find nose piercings, Mohawks, and some of the most outrageous clubbing clothes anywhere in the world, but strange items you never thought existed. Keep in mind, though, this especially trendy, touristy and commercial area can get very crowded.

Before leaving, be sure to check out one of London's most beautiful streets - the area on Regent's Park Road between King Henry's Road and Primrose Hill Road, near the Chalk Farm tube station. Here you can enjoy a quick meal or cup of tea at one of the many charming and moderately priced restaurants and coffee shops. Although the punks of Camden Town are long gone, the area has yet to feel too ritzy and posh.

## Brixton

Brixton, a unique and interesting neighborhood across the Thames in South London, is worth visiting. With a distinctly Caribbean flavor due to the

## ⟫Featured Hostels

### ST CHRISTOPHER'S INN - THE VILLAGE

161-165 Borough High St, *Southwark*
Dorms £10+; T: London Bridge
(207-939-9710)
www.st-christophers.co.uk/london
*This is the flagship London Hostel complete with a nightclub, Belushi's bar and a comedy club. A stone's throw from the attractions of the South Bank, including the London Eye, the Tate Modern, Shakespeare's Globe Theatre.*

### ST CHRISTOPHER'S INN SHEPHERD'S BUSH

28 Hammersmith Bway, *Hammersmith*
Dorms £10+; T: Shepherd's Bush
(not Shepherd's Bush Green)
(208-735-0270)
www.st-christophers.co.uk/london
*When you stay at this Hostel in London you're guaranteed a good time. No other London Youth Hostel is closer to the deafening beauty that is The 02 Shepherd's Bush Empire and no other London Hostel is closer to the biggest shopping centre in Europe - Westfield, just over the road.*

### ST CHRISTOPHER'S INN - THE INN

161-165 Borough High St, *Southwark*
Dorms £10+; T: Hammersmith
(207-407-2392)
www.st-christophers.co.uk/london
*Check out this London Hostel and Gastro Pub with a menu packed full of fresh food, from the nearby Borough Market. Take a trip through the market stalls and visit Sir Francis Drake's old ship - The Golden Hind and the London Dungeon.*

huge numbers of immigrants, Reggae music is always in the air as well as a more laid back, Caribbean attitude and energy.

Most of the life is squeezed into the triangle between Atlantic Road, Coldharbour Lane, and Brixton Road. Along these streets, you will find the area's pulsating market and many great pubs, cafés, and restaurants. Along **Coldharbour Lane**, in particular, there are various interesting and distinctive shops. Also take the time to walk further south along Brixton Hill Road and Atlantic Road, as well as along Brighton Terrace.

### Covent Garden, Piccadilly Circus & Soho

Take the tube to Covent Garden or Charing Cross to experience these delightfully bustling neighborhoods featuring shops, bars, restaurants, bright lights and lively entertainment.

### Ⓕ Historical Walk

If you want to see many of London's historical structures, start at the Tower of London near the Tower Bridge and Great Tower Street (Tower Bridge tube station) and walk along the Thames River. Along the way, you will pass St. Paul's Cathedral, Trafalgar Square, the Horse Guards, 10 Downing Street (of James Bond fame), Westminster Abbey, the Cabinet War Rooms, the Houses of Parliament and Big Ben to name a few. When you get to the Cabinet War Rooms, you can take a detour down Birdcage Walk to Buckingham Palace.

### ▸▸ Museums
### Ⓕ Tate Gallery of Modern Art

This converted old power plant is now one of the most impressive art museums in the world. The work housed here is a stunning compilation of modern works. As impressive as the art is the fantastic writing that accompanies the various exhibits. Open 10am to 6pm Sun-Thurs (tp 10pm Fri-Sat) and best of all, it is **free** (except for major exhibits). Take the tube to Southwark station. www.tate.org.uk

### Ⓕ National Gallery

Harboring one of Europe's greatest collections of paintings by masters such as Rembrandt and Van Gogh, this gallery is a classic staple. Open Monday to Saturday 10am-5pm, Sun 11-6pm. Free admission. Take the tube to Charing Cross. www.nga.gov

### ▸▸ Theatre

### Ⓢ Discounted Tickets

Discounted, same-day performance theatre tickets are available at the **Half-Price Ticket Booth**. Located in the clocktower building in Leicester Square. Open M-S, 10am-7pm, and Sun 11am-4pm. T: Leicester Square or Piccadilly Circus. www.txts.co.uk

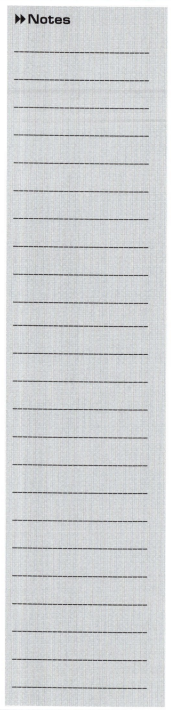

▸▸ Notes

# ▸Edinburgh

**EDINBURGH** quite gracefully and deservedly holds its title as the capital of Scotland. Named after old King Edwin of the 12th century, this now cosmopolitan city is a juxtaposition of a youthful artistic culture against a backdrop of hundreds of historical architectural landmarks sitting on the base of the magnificent Firth of Forth. It is during the month of August that the brilliance of Scotland's artistic talent shines when the Edinburgh Festival/Fringe Festival takes hold of the city. Thousands of tourists flock to Edinburgh to experience this unique and vibrant community.

## ▸Getting There

Edinburgh is an hour's drive west of Glasgow and a 4-hour rail trip (6-7hrs by bus) north of London. See **pages 8-11** for tours and transport to and from Edinburgh and Scotland.

### ▸From the Airport

The **Airlink** operates between Edinburgh Airport and Waverly Bridge in the city centre (next to the main railway station) and costs £3.50 o/w or £6 r/t. Buses operate 24hrs, every 20 minutes during the day and every 30-60 minutes other times. The trip takes 25 minutes. www.flybybus.com

### ▸Coach

National Express/Eurolines buses arrive and depart from the **St. Andrews Square Bus Station** located on Clyde Street near Princes Street in the city centre.

### ▸Rail

The main railway station is **Waverly**, located in Edinburgh's city centre, where trains arrive from both Scotland and England. Glasgow trains operate out of **Edinburgh Haymarket Station**.

## ▸Getting Around

### Lothian Regional Transport
Operates an extensive network of buses including night buses that kick in at midnight until approximately 4am. Single, adult bus fares (£1.40) are for one journey of any distance. You must have exact fare when boarding the bus. A **day ticket** costs just £3.50 for unlimited travel during the day. www.lothianbuses.co.uk

The **Edinburgh City Sightseeing Tour** is an open top, hop-on, hop-off, city tour for £12 for 24 hours. The ticket also gives you discounts such as 10% off Edinburgh Castle admission.

## ▸Visitor Info
www.edinburgh.org
See page 98 for Edinburgh city map.

## ▸Quick Facts
**Calling Information**
*Country Code*: 44

*Calling in the UK*: add a "0" before the area code

*Calling overseas*: 00+country code+area code+number

**Currency & Exchange Rates**
*Currency*: Scottish Pound (£)

*Currency Breakdown*:
100 Pence equals £1

*Exchange Rates*: £1 costs: US$1.61/ €1.24/ AUD$1.53/CAN$1.59

**Must See/Must Do**
Royal Mile, International Festival (Late August), Firth of Forth

**Say What!**
Beautiful=Bonnie as in "Bonnie Scotland." That's all we could bleeping understand!

## ▸Notes

----------------------------

----------------------------

----------------------------

----------------------------

----------------------------

----------------------------

----------------------------

----------------------------

----------------------------

----------------------------

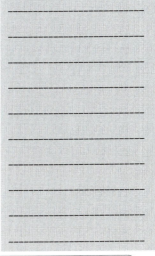

## ▶Things to See & Do

### ▶Tourist Information
The tourist info center is located at 3 Princes Street at Waverly Market. It's open daily from 9am-6pm (8pm in Summer). A smaller office is located at the airport.

### ▶Tours
### Ⓕ MacBackpackers Old Town Walking Tour
Free tours depart daily from 8 Blackfriars Street and go from Edinburgh Castle down to the Royal Palace.

### Ⓕ Royal Mile Walking Tour
MacBackpackers offers a free walking tour of the Royal Mile which leaves daily from their High Street Hostel at 8 Blackfriars Street.

### ▶Areas & Attractions
#### Royal Mile
The Royal Mile is the oldest part of Edinburgh and runs from **Edinburgh Castle** at its western end to the **Palace of Holyroodhouse**. In this area you will find traditional pubs, crowded tenements and cobblestone streets.

#### Edinburgh Castle
The Edinburgh Castle dates back to 850BC and sits atop a volcanic site known as **Castle Rock**. The castle is located at the western end of Royal Mile and is currently home to the Scottish division of the UK army. www.edinburghcastle.gov.uk

#### Calton Hill
Although only 330 feet high, this hill provides a great vantage point of Edinburgh, including views of Edinburgh Castle, Princes Street and the Firth of Forth.

#### Gladstone's Land
Once a townhouse community dating back to the 1600's, these restored homes are open to the public daily from 10am-5pm April-June/Sept-Oct (to 6:30pm July-Aug). Admission £6. Located along the Royal Mile. www.nts.org.uk/Property/Gladstones-Land

#### Ⓕ The Writer's Museum (Lady Stair's House)
Next to the Gladstone Lands, this museum houses the works of Scottish greats such as Sir Walter Scott, Robert Burns and Robert Louis Stevenson. Open daily, 10am-5pm.

## ▶Food & Nightlife
Edinburgh is not only swarming with pubs and bars, but is also chock full of charming and affordable multi-ethnic restaurants. For a night out, head to **Rose Street** or **Grassmarket Street** and you'll find tons of good restaurants and fun, lively pubs and bars to pass the night away.

## ▶Featured Hostels
Most hostels are central and within walking distance of the stations. Dorm prices range from £10-15. See **page 111** for a key to hostel icons

### ST CHRISTOPHER'S INN EDINBURGH
9-13 Market Street
Dorms £10+; T: Opposite Edinburgh Train Station. (131-226-1446)
www.st-christophers.co.uk/edinburgh
*This Edinburgh youth hostel is every backpacker's dream. With bright, airy rooms you'll have tons of space to stretch out. Located in the heart of the Old Town you're always where you want to be plus a built in bar and restaurant.*

### SMART CITY HOSTELS
50 Blackfriars Street
Dorms £14+; T: Waverly Train Station. (131-524-1989)
www.smartcityhostels.com
*Located in the heart of Edinburgh's Old Town, Smart City Hostels redefines the hostel experience. Bar 50, a fully licensed restaurant and bar, is located on the ground floor. And all of Edinburgh's famed attractions and lively night scene are right on our doorstep.*

## ▶Additional Hostels
**Castlerock Hostel**
15 Johnstone Terrace
(0131-225-9666)

**Edinburgh Backpackers**
65 Cockburn Street
(0131-221-1717)

**Edinburgh Bruntsfield YHA**
7 Bruntsfield Crescent
(0131-447-2994)

**Edinburgh Eglinton YHA**
18 Eglinton Crescent.
(0131-337-1120)

**Globetrotters Inn**
46 Marine Drive
(0131-336-1030)

**Royal Mile Hostel**
105 High Street
(0131-557-6120)

# ▶Glasgow

**GLASGOW** is the largest city in Scotland. More energetic, down to earth and inviting than its sister city, Edinburgh, Glasgow is a growing urban center that depicts Scottish culture, charm, and wit. As in Edinburgh, there exists a lively artistic community, exhibited in the many festivals it hosts. With interesting gothic architecture, a developing city center and proximity to the gorgeous Highlands, stop in for some authentic Scottish hospitality and you won't be disappointed.

## ▶Getting There

Glasgow is an hour's drive east of Edinburgh and a 4.5-hour rail trip (8hrs by bus) north of London.

### ▶From the Airport

**Glasgow Airport** 8 miles south west of the city. From stand 1, the Glasgow Shuttle runs every 10 minutes, 24hrs, for £5o/w. **Glasgow Prestwick** airport is located 22 miles (35km) to the south-west of Glasgow. From here, you can catch the train to Glasgow Central Station every 30 minutes (50smin, from £6.40 o/w) or to Edinburgh via Glasgow (2hrs 15mins, from £14.70).

### ▶Coach & Rail

The main station is **Buchanan Bus Station** located on Killermont Street in central Glasgow. **Central Station** handles trains to England and southern Scotland. **Queen Street Station** services trains to northern Scotland. Both stations are within walking distance of each other and centrally located.

## ▶Getting Around

Glasgow is easily and best explored by foot. The **Underground** costs £1.20/trip or £3.50/day (valid after 9:30am, Mon.-Sat). A **Roundabout Ticket**, which provides unlimited travel to over 110 country stations as well as the Underground, costs £6, valid after 9am M-F and all day on weekends.

## ▶Things to See & Do

The main tourist info center is located at 11 George Square. Areas to check out include the **Southside**, **West End**, **Old Town**, **East End**, **Merchant City**, **George Square** and the area around the **Glasgow Cathedral**. Attractions to check out include **Tenement House**, the free **Gallery of Modern Art**, the highly regarded (and also free) **Burrell Collection** and **Barras**, Glasgow's street market. The place to go for pubs and pub crawls is **Byres Road**, located in the West End.

## ▶Visitor Info

www.seeglasgow.com

## ▶Quick Facts

**Calling Information**
*Country Code*: 44

*Calling in the UK*: add a "0" before the area code

*Calling overseas*: 00+country code+area code+number

**Currency & Exchange Rates**
*Currency*: Scottish Pound (£)

*Currency Breakdown*:
100 Pence equals £1

*Exchange Rates*: £1 costs: US$1.61/ €1.24/ AUD$1.53/CAN$1.59

## ▶Hostels

**Blue Sky Hostel**
65 Berkeley Street
(0141-221-1710)

**Euro Hostels**
318 Clyde Street
(0141-222-2828)

**Glasgow Backpackers**
17 Park Terrace
(0141-332-9099)

**Glasgow YHA**
7/8 Park Terrace
(0141-332-3004)

## ▶Notes

_____

_____

_____

_____

_____

_____

# ▸▸Dublin

DUBLIN has become a major European center, now known for its youthful culture, rich history, vibrant pubs and cosmopolitan restaurants. With its stunning nearby countryside, it is an inviting and friendly city that serves as an excellent place to start and finish your European journey.

## ▸▸Getting There

See **pages 8-11** for tours and transport to and from Dublin and other parts of Ireland.

### ▸▸From the Airport

You can take either the local city bus or the **Airlink 747** into the city. The Airlink 747 Coach Service, which goes to the main bus station and to the Connolly and Heuston train terminals, runs approximately every fifteen minutes from 7:15am-11:30pm daily, costs €6 o/w, €10 r/t and takes 30-50 minutes. The **local bus** (41, 41b) takes you to Lower Abby Street from 6am-11:30pm daily, costs €2.20 and takes about 30 minutes. www.dublinbus.ie

### ▸▸Coach

**Busarus**, the main bus station, is located on Store Street opposite the Connolly Rail Station. Eurolines and the Irish national bus line, Bus Éirrean, arrive and depart from here.

### ▸▸Rail

There are two train stations in Dublin that service different locations throughout Ireland. **Connolly Station** on Amiens Street in Central Dublin operates trains to Northern Ireland, including Belfast and places in the north of Ireland.

If you are coming from or going to the south and west, including to/from Cork and Galway, you need to go to **Heuston Station** on St John's Road West.

**Iarnród Éireann (Irish Rail)** is Ireland's national rail service that operates intercity rail services throughout Ireland and Northern Ireland. If booked on their website, fares are: Dublin to Galway €15+ each way and Dublin to Cork €20+ each way. www.irishrail.ie

### ▸▸Ferry

Ferry service to Dublin and other parts of Ireland and Northern Ireland are available from a number of locations in England, Scotland and Wales. Ferries to Dublin arrive at **Dún Laoghaire** (from here, take the DART to Dublin Connolly Station) or **Dublin Ferryport** (from here, take Dublin Bus # 53 to central Dublin). Ferry service takes from 1 hour on high-speed ferries to 3 ½ hours. www.irishferries.com

## ▸▸Visitor Info

www.visitdublin.com

See page 99 for Dublin city map.

## ▸▸Quick Facts

**Calling Information**

*Country Code*: 353

*Calling in Ireland*: add a "0" before the area code

*Calling overseas*: 00+country code+area code+number

**Currency & Exchange Rates**

*Currency*: Euro (€)

*Currency Breakdown*:
100 cents equals €1

*Exchange Rates*: €1 costs: US$1.30/ £.81/AUD$1.24/ CAN$1.28

**Must See/Must Do**

Irish Pubs; Irish Wit; Irish Countryside; Belfast

**Say What!**

What's happening=What's the craic; I drank 15 pints of Guinness last night!=D'ol me cuig deag Guinness areir; Cheers=Slainte

## »Getting Around

### Dublin Bus

Dublin Bus operates throughout the greater Dublin area to and from the Dublin city centre. Fares are based on stages traveled and range from €1.25 (1-3 stages) to €2.40 (over 23 stages). A **Dublin Rambler** ticket provides unlimited bus travel for €6.50 (1 day), €14.20 (3 days) or €23 (5 days). For €11.75, the 1-day **Shorthop** Bus/Rail Pass provides unlimited off-peak travel on bus, suburban rail and DART (Dublin Area Rapid Transport). www.dublinbus.ie

**Nitelink** night buses depart from various locations in the city centre every Thurs-Sat nights at 12:30am, 1:30am, 2:30am, 3:30am and 4:30am and cost €5.

### DART Rail

The DART can take you around the greater Dublin area to visit beaches, villages and other attractions. Fares are based on distance and and range from €1.35 to €4.35. www.irishrail.ie

## »Things to See & Do

### »Tourist Information

The tourist info center is located on Suffolk Street.

### »Tours

### Bus Tours of Dublin

Hop-on, hop-off bus tours of the city are an excellent way to explore Dublin. Most tours include about 12 stops and cover most of Dublin's attractions. The **Dublin City Tour** ticket costs €18 and leaves from 59 Upper O'Connell Street daily. **Guide Friday** and **The Old Dublin Tour** costs about the same but include an additional stop. Most tours last from 75 to 90 minutes.

### Belfast Day Tour

Leaves at 8am from Dublin and costs €45. Optional Black Taxi Tour through Belfast can be included. Operated by Paddywagon Tours. (01-823-0882)

### Guinness Storehouse

A visit to Ireland is not complete without a Guinness brewery tour and, of course, a pint of true Guinness (included in the €14.85 admission price, students €13). Located on Crane Street and open daily. www.guinness-storehouse.com

### Walking Tours

There are several fun and interesting walking tours that unmask the city's character and its players. On the **Traditional Irish-Music Pub Crawl** (www.discoverdublin.ie/musical-pub-crawl) you are guided by two musicians to several pubs while drinking Guinness and listening to them play Irish music. **The Literary Pub Crawl** (www.dublinpubcrawl.com)

## »Featured Hostels

See **page 111** for a key to hostel icons.

### AVALON HOUSE

55 Aungier Street
Dorms €10+; Private €20+ pp
(01-475-0001)
www.avalon-house.ie
*One of Dublin's most ideally located budget accommodation centres! Shop all day on Dublin's main shopping street, enjoy the scenery in one of Europe's most beautiful parks, relax in a vast selection of restaurants or museums.*

### KINLAY HOUSE DUBLIN

2/12 Lord Edward Street
Dorms €10+; Private €20+ pp
(01-679-6644)
www.kinlaydublin.ie
*In the famous Temple Bar district, Kinlay House is only minutes from the best selection of Dublin's bars, cafes, restaurants and within easy walking distance to all Dublin's top attractions including Dublin Castle.*

## »Additional Hostels

**Abbey Hostel**
29 Bachelors Walk
(01-878-0700)

**Barnacle's Temple Bar**
19 Temple Lane
(01-671-6277)

**Four Courts Hostel**
15-17 Merchant's Quay
(01-672-5839)

**Generator Hostel**
Smithfield Square
(01-874-2424)

**Globetrotters Tourist Hostel**
46 Lower Gardiner Street
(01-873-5893)

**Oliver St John Gogarty**
18-21 Anglesea Street
(01-671-1822)

**Paddy's Palace**
5 Beresford Place. L. Gardner Street (01-888-1756)

similarly introduces you to actors spouting Yeats and Joyce in between a pint or two. The non-alcoholic and more studious tour is given by **Historical Walking Tours of Dublin** (www.historicalinsights.ie). All tours last approximately two hours and cost between €10-13.

## ▶Areas & Attractions

### Ⓕ National Museum of Ireland
This free museum offers a glimpse as far back as the Bronze Age with ancient Viking artifacts and Bronze age Irish gold on display. Located on Kildare Street and is open daily except Monday. DART: Pearse Street. www.museum.ie

### Trinity College & Library
Trinity College was founded in 1592 by Elizabeth I and is one of the most important sites historically for Dublin in terms of architecture. Of special interest is the **"Book of Kells"** on display in the Old Library. The book dates back to 800AD and is one of the oldest in the world. The Old Library is open daily and costs about €9. Take the DART to Pearse Street (closed Sundays). www.tcd.ie/Library

### Ⓕ Leinster House
Built in the late 1700s, Leinster House has been home to the Irish Parliament since 1922. You can get free tickets to watch parliamental debates if you are in Dublin when Parliament is in session. Located on Kildare Street. DART: Pearse Street. www.oireachtas.ie

### Ⓕ Irish Museum of Modern Art
This museum housed inside a former hospital was built in the late 17th century. It's open daily and is free. At Royal Hospital, Military Road, Kilmainham. www.imma.ie

### Kilmainham Gaol
Between 1796 and 1924, thousands of Irish prisoners fighting for independence from Britain were executed and held prisoner within these damp gray prison walls. The cost of €6 includes an audio visual tour. Located on Inchcore Road and open daily. www.heritageireland.ie/en/Dublin/KilmainhamGaol

## ▶Food & Nightlife

Many pubs have good traditional food at great prices. In particular check out the **Temple Bar** area. It's touristy but great for a good pint and cheap places to eat. Definitely check out the Brazen Head, the oldest pub in Dublin at 20 Lower Bridge Street.

## ▶City Escapes

### Malahide & Howth
Get away to these coastal towns, each with a castle to check out. Located south of Dublin, both towns offer nice beaches and are about 30 minutes away by DART.

## ▶Notes

# ▶▶Benelux Region

**(Netherlands, Belgium, Luxembourg)**

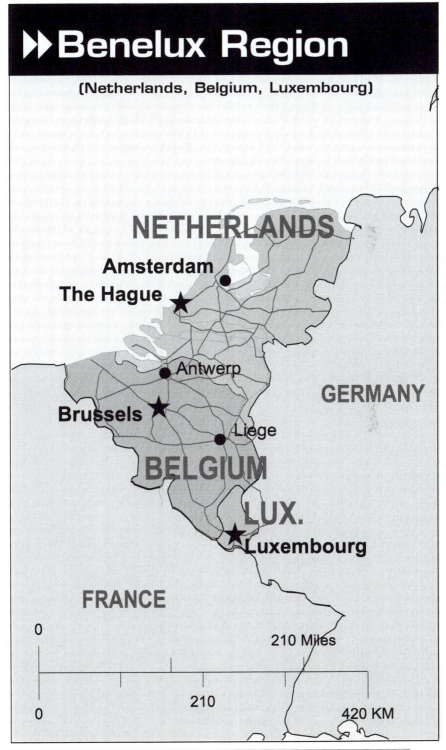

NETHERLANDS

Amsterdam

The Hague

Antwerp

GERMANY

Brussels

Liege

BELGIUM

LUX.

Luxembourg

FRANCE

0

210 Miles

210

0

420 KM

# ▸Belgium

## ▸Brussels

Known for its chocolate, beer and waffles, Brussels is not as picturesque as Bruges or exciting as Amsterdam. But, this thousand year old city is fast becoming a multi-cultural center as people from all over the world have taken up residence here, including a large French speaking African culture. Filled with its historic buildings, cobblestone streets, and crowded alehouses, it's worth a stop over. **To See/Do**: Musee D'Art Moderne, Grand Place, Bourse, Manneken Pis.

## ▸Antwerp

Once the premier center of Flemish art and culture, Antwerp today simultaneously offers her visitors a glance into the golden baroque age of past centuries while providing an artistic haven for cutting edge contemporary culture. When exploring the historic narrow, winding streets take in the great masterpieces of artists such as Rubens and Van Dyke, browse through countless modern galleries and shops and gawk at the world-famous diamond district. When you're finished, you can turn in any direction to find a friendly pub or alehouse. Take a nap, then head towards the dizzying and much celebrated club scene. **To See/Do**: Rubenshuis, Royal Museum of Fine Arts, Diamantmuseum (€6) and Grote Markt area.

## ▸Bruges

One of the most visited cities in Belgium, you'll feel as if you stepped onto a medieval film set. Bruges' medieval architecture and character is perfectly preserved and invites many visitors. But don't let that deter you from exploring its ancient streets, acclaimed museums and tons of fun pubs and cafés. **To See/Do**: Groeninge Museum, Markt and Burg squares, bike tour.

# ▸Luxembourg

The tiny country of Luxembourg, situated between Belgium, France and Germany, sits amidst idyllic natural beauty and glorious architecture. With a history dating back to the Romans, Luxembourg offers a taste of old Europe: castles and grand squares are complemented by the wealth of modern-day architecture and popular culture. **To See/Do**: Palais Grand-Ducal, Countryside: Moselle Valley (wineries), Vianden and Echternach.

# ▸Netherlands

## ▸Rotterdam/Utrecht

Lying south of Amsterdam, these two Randstadt cities are distinctly different from other quaint old-

# ▸Visitor Info

**Belgium:**
www.visitbelgium.com
**Netherlands:**
www.visitholland.com

# ▸Quick Facts

**Calling Information**
*Country Code*: Belgium 32; Holland 31

*Calling from within*: add a "0" before the area code

*Calling overseas*: 00+country code+area code+number

**Currency & Exchange Rates**
*Currency*: Euro (€)

*Currency Breakdown*:
100 cents equals €1

*Exchange Rates*: €1 costs: US$1.30/ £.81/AUD$1.24/ CAN$1.28

# ▸Featured Hostels

See **page 111** for a key to hostel icons.

**ST CHRISTOPHER'S INN BRUGES**
133-137 Langestraat, *Bruges*
Dorms €15+; T: Bus #6 or #16 from main train station. (32-50-34-10-93)
www.st-christophers.co.uk/bruges
*This trendy central hostel has everything you need: cybercafe, bike rentals, and the ever popular Bauhaus Bar where you can work your way through Belgium's very tasty selection of over 450 beers.*

# ▸Belgium Hostels

**New Int'l Youth Hotel**
Provinciestraat 256, *Antwerp*
(323-230-0522)

**Herdersbrug Youth Hostel**
Louis Coiseaukaai 46, *Bruge*
(050-59-93-21)

**Hostel Lybeer**
Korte Vulderstraat 31, *Bruge*
(050-33-43-55)

**Snuffel Sleep In**
Ezelstraat 47-49, *Bruge*
(050-33-31-33)

**Bruegel Youth Hostel (HI)**
Heilige Geeststraat 2, *Brussels*
(02-511-0436)

world Dutch towns. After being destroyed in WWII, Rotterdam was re-built as a thoroughly modern city with glass and steel skyscrapers. Utrecht, although surrounded by an historic brick wall, is also marked by the development of contemporary architecture and infrastructure. However, both cities are still visited by many tourists who enjoy the range of historic monuments, museums, bars, cafés and restaurants (especially in Utrecht). **To See/Do: Rotterdam**: Boymans-Van Beuningen Museum, Delfshaven. **Utrecht**: Dom Tower, Catharijneconvent Museum.

## ▶The Hague (Den Haag)

The Hague, a popular beach town and home to Holland's Queen Beatrix, will enchant you with its colorful mix of culture, history and natural beauty. Just a 45-minute train ride from Amsterdam, it offers an ideal change of pace for a day trip. You can tour the royal stables or the Peace Palace that seats the famous International Court of Justice, and then explore the Maurithaus museum, which presides over a shimmering canal and houses Johannes Vermeer's "Girl with Pearl Earring." Stop by one of the various flea markets or hang out at a smokers' "coffeeshop." Wander down to Scheveningen and stroll along its beautiful wide beaches and Victorian promenade which becomes a hopping club scene at night. For in-town nightlife, check out the bars and cafés in the "historic passage" and around the square. Must see/do: Maurithaus, M.C. Escher museum, Scheveningen (the beach district)

## ▶Notes

_____

_____

_____

_____

_____

_____

_____

_____

**Center Vincent Van Goh**
Travesiere 8, *Brussels*
(02-217-0158)

**Generation Europe
Youth Hostel**
4, Rue de l'Éléphant, *Brussels*
(02-410-3858)

**Jacques Brel Youth Hostel**
30 Rue de la Sablonnière, *Brussels.*
(02-218-0187)

**Sleepwell Youth Hostel**
Rue du Damier 23, *Brussels*
(02-218-5050)

## ▶Netherlands Hostels

For Amsterdam hostels, see page 33.

**Stayokay Arnhem**
Diepenbrocklaan 27, *Arnhem*
(026-442-0114)

**Stayokay Utrecht-Bunnik**
Rhijnauwenselaan 14, *Bunnik*
(030-656-1277)

**Stayokay Den Haag**
Scheepmakersstraat 27, *Den Haag*
(070-315-7888)

**Stayokay Den Haarlem**
Jan Gijzenpad 3, *Haarlem*
(023-537-3793)

**Stayokay Maastricht**
Maasboulevard 101, *Maastricht*
(043-750-17 90)

**Sleep-In**
Mauritsweg 29b, *Rotterdam*
(010-414-3256)

**Stayokay Rotterdam**
Rochussenstraat 107-109, *Rotterdam*
(010-436-5763)

**Stayokay Soest**
Bosstraat 16, *Soest*
(035-601-2296)

**B+B Utrecht**
Egelantierstraat 25, *Utrecht*
(650-434-884)

**B+B Utrecht City Centre**
Lucasbolwerk 4, *Utrecht*
(650-434-884)

**Strowis Hostel**
Boothstraat 8, *Utrecht*
(030-238-0280)

# ▸▸Amsterdam

**AMSTERDAM** is a wonderful and interesting city that entices every traveler with more than just its indulgent drug laws and liberal, carefree society. Its splendid canals, bridges and architecture envelop the city with charm and lend to its rich artistic history and culture. Its bars, cafés, galleries and numerous forms of entertainment also make this one of the best party towns.

With a relatively small urban base it is easily discovered, especially if you rent a bike and take advantage of the well maintained bike paths to the outskirts of the city. Most attractions, museums and hotspots are within walking distance of Centraal Station.

## ▸▸Getting There

For info on tours and transport see **pages 8-11**.

Amsterdam is about 300 miles north of Paris, 365 miles west of Berlin, 125 miles north of Brussels and 45 miles north of Rotterdam.

### ▸▸From the Airport

**Schiphol Airport** is one of Europe's best airports and is only 11 miles south west of Amsterdam. The cheapest option from the airport is the rail from Schiphol Plaza to Centraal Station. It takes 15-20 minutes and costs only €3.80 2nd class, €6.50 1st class. Trains operate very frequently, 24 hours per day. www.schiphol.nl

### ▸▸Coach & Rail

**Eurolines** buses depart from the bus terminal outside **Amstel Station**. You can take the metro five stops from Centraal Station to get there. **Eurail** and **Thalys** trains arrive and depart from **Amsterdam Centraal Station** where you can walk to your hostel, rent a bike or catch a tram. The **Eurostar** from London arrives in Brussels where you can easily catch connecting trains to Amsterdam Centraal Station.

## ▸▸Getting Around

Amsterdam is a great place to walk or rent a bike to get around and see the sights. Alternatively, you can take the trams, trains, buses and metro operated by the **GVB**. The buses and metro are mostly for suburban traffic. However, the metro is useful for traveling between Centraal Station and Amstel Station.

## ▸▸Visitor Info

www.iamsterdam.com

See page 100 for Amsterdam city map

## ▸▸Quick Facts

**Calling Information**
*Country Code*: 31

*Calling in Holland*: add a "0" before the area code

*Calling overseas*: 00+country code+area code+number

**Currency & Exchange Rates**
*Currency*: Euro (€)

*Currency Breakdown*:
100 cents equals €1

*Exchange Rates*: €1 costs: US$1.30/ £.81/AUD$1.24/ CAN$1.28

**Must See/Must Do**
Rent a bike, Red Light District, Canal boat ride

**Say What!**
Where is=Waar is de... ; How much is it=Hoeveel kost het?;Do you speak English=Spreek je Engels; I'd like=Ik wil graag;Do you have=Heeft u...?

## ▸▸Notes

_____

_____

_____

_____

_____

_____

_____

The metro runs from 6am-12:15am M-F (from 6:30am Sat, 7:30am Sun).Trams and buses start at the same time and go to midnight. After midnight, the night buses kick in and all go to and from Centraal Station.

To ride the trams, buses and trains you must purchase an OV-chipkaart (PT Smart Card), which is the new system to pay for public transport in Amsterdam and all of the Netherlands. You can add funds to the OV-chipkaart and pay per use, which costs €2.70 for a 1-hour card.

You can also purchase cards for 1-day (€7.50), 2-day (€12), 3-day (€16), 4-day (€20.50), 5-day (€25), 6-day (€28.50) or 7-day (€31). www.gvb.nl

### ⤐ Bike Rental

There are many bike rental companies. Check around Centraal Station. Rentals cost about €12-15 per day and usually require a deposit of €20-50.

## ⤐ Things to See & Do

### ⤐ Tourist Information

The tourist info center (VVV) is located at Stationsplein 10 (9-5 daily), platform 2 of Centraal Station and Leidseplein 1.

### ⤐ Tours
#### Canal Cruises

A number of cruises are available from outside Centraal Station and cost about €14 for a 1-hour tour and depart every 15 minutes. You can rent a peddleboat and take your own canal cruise.

#### Mike's Bike Tours

Take a guided 3-4 hour bicycle tour and get to know the city and countryside the Dutch way. Tours leave daily from West Entrance of the Rijksmuseum €19-22. www.mikesbiketoursamsterdam.com

#### Ⓕ IJ Ferry

This free ferry from Centraal Station travels across the IJ River. It's worth the trip if you don't want to pay for a canal cruise.

#### Ⓢ Walking & Biking Tours

You can pick up walking tour guides at the VVV for €2-4. Also check out the VVV for complete bus and bicycle tour guides.

### ⤐ Areas & Attractions

The **Amsterdam Card** is available for 1 (€40), 2 (€50) or 3 (€60) days. The pass includes a Transportation Ticket and 50 free admissions and 60 discounted admissions to major tourist attractions and restaurants. The Amsterdam Card is available from the local tourist information offices.

### ⤐ Featured Hostels

See **page 111** for a key to hostel icons

#### ST CHRISTOPHER'S INN

129 Warmoesstraat
Dorms €15+; T: Near Amsterdam
Train Station. (206-231-380)
www.st-christophers.co.uk/amsterdam
*St Christopher's at the Winston offers all en-suite rooms, a private beer garden outside or our shiny new Belushi's bar, a built in nightclub at the famous Winston International and a chill-out room for some quiet time.*

#### THE FLY PIG UPTOWN

Vossiusstraat 46
Dorms €15+; T: Tram 2 or5 to
Rijks Museum . (204-004-187)
www.flyingpig.nl
*Right in the middle of Amsterdam - next to the Leidseplein, a square famous for the many clubs and pubs and overlooking the Vondelpark. Known for our great mix of a relaxed and funky atmosphere, and the real Amsterdam party vibe!*

#### THE FLY PIG DOWNTOWN

Nieuwendijk 100
Dorms €15+; T: walk from Amsterdam
Central Station. (204-206-822)
www.flyingpig.nl
*Next to Amsterdam Central Station and the Red Light District. This 18th century building has been transformed into one of the best party spots in Amsterdam! We are known for our wild nights and a relaxed atmosphere, mixed in with all the comforts of home!*

### ⤐ Add'l Hostels

#### The Bulldog

Oudezijds Voorburgwal 220, *Old City Centre*. (020-620-3822)

#### The Flying Pig Beach Hostel

Parallel Boulevard 208,
*Noordwijk*
(071-362-2533)

#### Hans Brinker

Kerkstraat 136, *Leidseplein*
(020-622-0687)

## Van Gogh Museum
Houses a chronological collection of Van Gogh's work as well as other artists. Open daily from 9am-5pm and costs €17.50. Paulus Potterstraat 7. T: 2, 5 from Centraal Station. www.vangoghmuseum.nl

## Red Light District
A visit to Amsterdam is not complete without checking out the oldest area in town! Here you will not only find interesting museums - **Hash Marijuana Hemp Museum** (148 Oudezides Achterburgwal), and **Tattoo Museum** (Oudezijds Achterburgwal 130) but the **Condomerie** (condom shop) at Warmoesstraat 141. T: 4, 9, 14, 16, 24, 25 to Nieuwemarkt.

## Dam Square
A five minute walk south of Centraal Station, this was the site of the first dam built across the Amstel River back in the 13th century. It is also home to the **Sex Museum** at Damrak 18, the **Torture Museum** at Damrak 20 and the Royal Palace. Dam Square is about a 1/4 mile walk from Centraal Station along Damrak. T: 1, 2, 4, 5, 9, 13, 14, 16, 17, 20, 24, 25.

## ⑤ Heineken Experience
Four levels of interactive experiences in the former brewery and free beer. Tours are available daily from 11am-7:30pm with last ticket sales at 5:30pm. Admission, including free beer, is €17 at the door or €15 if purchased online. Get there early - tours fill up fast. Stadhouderskade 78. T: 6, 7, 10, 16, 24 or 25. www.heinekenexperience.com

## Floating Flower Market
The **Bloemenmarkt** is located on the Singel Canal at the top end of the Leidseplein at the Muntplein (Mint Tower). A beautiful sight to see and smell. Open daily 9am-5:30pm, Sunday 11am-5:30pm.

## Ⓕ Westerkerk
A protestant church with the tallest tower in Amsterdam and reputed burial place of Rembrandt. It's free to get in. Open daily 11am-3pm except Sunday. Prinsengracht 281. www.westerkerk.nl

## ▶▶Food & Nightlife
Amsterdam is hopping with cool, hip bars and cafés, especially in **Leidseplein** and **Rembrandtplein**. Also, check out the more low key, authentic Jordaan area. For the latest happenings in English, pick up *Time Out Magazine*.

▶▶Notes

# France

ENGLAND

London ★  Amsterdam ★

NETHERLANDS

Brussels ★

BELGIUM

GERMANY

Rennes ● Caen   Paris ★
Lorient ● Laval         Nancy ●
La Baule-
Escoublac ● Nantes ●
La Roche-
sur-Yon ●      Tours ●
                    Dijon ●
La Rochelle ● Poitiers ●          Zurich ●
Saintes ●                Lyon ●
Bay        Limoges ●   FRANCE   SWITZ.   AUSTRIA
of
Biscay     Bordeaux
                    Valence ●
SPAIN      Toulouse ●          ITALY
                Nimes ●
                    Marseilles ●

Barcelona ●   Mediterranean Sea

Rome ★

0        210        420 Miles
|————————|————————|————————|
0        210    420 KM

## ▶Loire Valley

About 100 miles southwest of Paris, sitting along the banks of the long, winding Loire river, the valley is mainly visited for its magnificent châteaux and castles. These grand structures are set amidst beautiful countryside that is dotted with quaint towns and villages such as Saumur, Chinon, Blois and Tours (university site). There are trains available that pass through each town, so you can tour the entire region via rail pass.

For the more athletically inclined, bicycling through this region is extremely popular and highly recommended as you can tour the many vineyards and wineries along the way. Bikes can be rented from some rail stations and in each town (ask at train station). **To See/Do: Blois**: Château de Blois, Château de Chambord; **Tours**: Château de Chenonceau, Château d'azay-le-Rideau. **Saumur**: wine tasting.

## ▶Dijon/Lyon/Mont Blanc

This region, southwest of Paris and north of Provence, is comprised of pretty, tranquil medieval towns that sit in the shadow of the stunning French Alps. Dijon is the most northern town, situated in the Burgundy region. It is a lively Renaissance city that is home to a large university and offers some of Burgundy's premier wineries in the nearby countryside. Lyon, known as the culinary capital of France, is a large flourishing modern city that still retains its medieval character in the old city section. Chamonix and Mont-Blanc sit at the foot of the French Alps enveloping you in stunning, picturesque scenery.

## ▶Provence

Comprised of picturesque towns such as Avignon, Arles, Marseille and Aix-en-Provence, this ancient region cultivated by the Romans is a world unto itself. Yes, it is often heavily touristed, but the juxtaposition of romance, country life, modern style and innovation has not detracted from Provence's historic character and seductive charm.

Visit wineries and lounge in tiny bistros in Aix-en-Provence. Bike ride through wildflowers and visit ancient attractions in medieval Arles. And indulge in sophisticated cafés in burgeoning Marseilles. Provence has always delighted her visitors! **To See/Do**: **Arles**: St-Triomphe Cloister; **Aix-en-Provence**: Cathedrale St-Sauveur, markets and cafés; **Avignon**: Palais de Papes; **Marseilles**: The Old Port, Le Panier.

## ▶Visitor Info

www.franceguide.com

## ▶Quick Facts

**Calling Information**
*Country Code*: 33

*Calling in France*: add a "0" before the area code

*Calling overseas*: 00+country code+area code+number

**Currency & Exchange Rates**
*Currency*: Euro (€)

*Currency Breakdown*:
100 cents=1 €

*Exchange Rates*: €1 costs: US$1.30/ £.81/AUD$1.24/ CAN$1.28

## ▶Highlights

Paris, Avignon, Aix-en-Provence, Loire Valley, Nice

## ▶Hostels Loire Valley

**Auberge de Jeunesse du Vieux Tours (HI)**
5, rue Bretonneau, *Tours*.
(02-47-37-81-58)

## ▶Hostels Dijon/ Lyon/Mont Blanc

**Chamonix Youth hostel (HI)**
127, Montée Jacq Balmat, *Chamonix Mont-Blanc* (04-50-53-14-52)

**Youth Hostel Vieux Lyon (HI)**
41-45, Montée du Chemin Neuf, *Lyon* (04-78-15-05-50)

**Centre Int'l de Sejour de Lyon**
103, Boulevard des Etats-Unis, *Lyon* (04-37-90-42-42)

## ▶Hostels Provence

**Youth Hostel Aix-en-Provence (HI)**
3, ave, Marcel Pagnol. *Aix-en-Provence* (04-42-20-15-99)

**Youth Hostel Arles (HI)**
20, avenue Foch, *Arles* (04-90-96-18-25)

**Youth Hostel Marseille "Bonneveine" (HI)**
Impasse Bonfils Ave., *Marseille* (04-91-17-63-30)

## ▸Cote d'Azur

Renowned for its sophistication, wealth and power, the Cote d'Azur is a tourist haven offering not just a golden St. Tropez tan, but a rich nightlife and natural beauty.

The more laid-back (relatively speaking) large town of Nice has lots of cafés, bars, markets and, of course, pebble beaches (take your flip-flops). Cannes and St. Tropez are better as day trips from Nice, as they are really over touristed millionaires' playgrounds - still fun to check out though, especially if there's a festival in town. **To See/Do**: Nice: Musee Matisse, Musee Chagall; **St. Tropez**: Musee de l'Annonciade.

## ▸Brittany

Brittany is France's more cultural and down-to-earth northwestern counterpart to the French Riviera in the south. And since it's just across the English Channel, it's a perfect stop on the way to or from Paris or London. The dramatic coastline with jagged cliffs and white sand beaches are just a precursor to the charming, lush Celtic towns of St. Malo, Quimper, Vannes, Dinan and the larger Rennes. Celtic pride and history is exhibited in the names, language and culture throughout the region. It is a distinctly different area from the rest of France. Go during one of the local festivals and you'll be treated to traditional costumes and festive activities. **To See/Do**: **St. Malo**: Château, Fort National; **Dinan**: Tour du Coëtquen; **Rennes**: Musée Des Beaux-Arts, Jardin Du Thabor.

## ▸Bordeaux

More than a delicious red wine, Bordeaux is a proud and historic city located in the Aquitaine region in the southwest of France. Walk along Les Quais on the shores of the Garonne River, cross the bridges or hop on a ferry for a unique view of the city. Hit the pedestrian center for shopping, dining and cultural pursuits and explore Bordeaux' many gardens, museums and cafes along with a bottle of – what else? Bordeaux.

## ▸Notes

_____

_____

_____

## ▸Hostels Cote d'Azur

**Iris Hostel**
77 Boulevard Carnot, *Cannes*
(04-93-68-30-20)

**Le Chalit**
27, Ave. Maréchal Galliéni, *Cannes*
(04-93-99-22-11)

**Auberge de Jeunesse – Nice (HI)**
Route Forestière du Mont-Alban, *Nice* (04-93-89-23-64)

**Backpackers Chez Patrick**
32 rue Pertinax fl 1, *Nice*
(04-93-80-30-72)

**Hotel Antares**
5 Av. Thiers, *Nice*
(04-93-88-22-87)

## ▸Hostels Brittany

**Auberge de Jeunesse (HI)**
37, ave. du R.P. Umbricht, B.P. 108, *St. Malo* (02-99-40-29-80)

**Auberge de Jeunesse (HI)**
10-12, Canal Saint Martin, *Rennes* (02-99-33-22-33)

**Auberge de Jeunesse (HI)**
Vallée de la Fontaine des Eaux, *Dinan* (02-96-39-10-83)

## ▸Hostels Strasbourg

**Auberge de Jeunesse Parc du Rhin (HI)**
Rue des Cavaliers B.P. 58, *Strasbourg* (03-88-45-54-20)

**Auberge de Jennesse Rene Cassin (HI)**
9 Rue de l'Auberge de Jeunesse, *Strasbourg* (03-88-30-26-46)

# ▶▶Paris

PARIS is stunning! Whether you indulge in its grand and monumental history or embrace its intimate romance, Parisian culture will leave its mark on you. Always elegant and pure in its "Frenchness", Paris gives you no doubt that you are in one of the greatest cities on earth. Explore the cozy cafés, buy coveted delicacies from the many markets and take in the essential sights. But be wary of your cash flow – like many other cities of its stature, Paris is not cheap!

## ▶Getting There

Paris is located in northern central France, 165 miles south west of Brussels, 300 miles south of Amsterdam and under 4 hours by rail from London via the Chunnel.

### ▶From the Airport
### Aéroport Charles de Gaulle

If you are flying internationally, you will likely use **Aéroport Charles de Gaulle** (CDG), located about 17 miles north of Paris. To get to the Paris city center, take the **RER Express Train** Line B from airport terminals 1 & 2 to either stations Gare du Nord (25 mins) or Denfert Rochereau (35 mins) in Paris. From there you can catch the **Métro** to your final destination.

If you purchase/have a **Carte Orange or Paris Visite Pass** valid to zone 5 (see below), your transport is covered. Otherwise the cost is €9.10 each way. Line B operates every 10-15 minutes on weekdays from 4:56am-11:56pm. When going to the airport, take the RER line B/Roissy-CDG.

Alternatively, you can take the **RATP Roissybus** (Paris public transport system bus) that operates between CDG and Opéra Garnier (corner of rue Scribe/rue Auber in the city). The Roissybus takes 45-60 minutes and costs €10. It operates daily, every 15-20 minutes from 6am-11pm. The RATP also accepts the Carte Orange or Paris Visite passes (if valid to zone 5 – see below). http://www.aeroportsdeparis.fr

### Aéroport d'Orly

To get to the city center, take the free shuttle bus from any terminal to station **Pont de Rungis-Aéroport d'Orly** and catch the RER (train) Line C2. The combined tickets costs €6.40 and takes about 35-45 minutes.

You can also use the Carte Orange or Paris Visite passes valid to zone 4. Trains run every 20 minutes from 5am-11:30 pm. The **RATP Orlybus** runs

## ▶Visitor Info

www.parisinfo.com

See page 101 for a Paris city map

## ▶Quick Facts

### Calling Information
*Country Code*: 33

*Calling in France*: add a "0" before the area code

*Calling overseas*: 00+country code+area code+number

### Currency & Exchange Rates
*Currency*: Euro (€)

*Currency Breakdown*:
100 cents equals €1

*Exchange Rates*: €1 costs: US$1.30/ £.81/AUD$1.24/ CAN$1.28

### Must See/Must Do
Eiffel Tower, Cabaret Show, Sidewalk Cafés

### Say What!
Where is=Ou est...; How much is it=C'est combien?; Do you speak English=Parlez-vous anglais? I'd like=Je voudrais...; Do you have=Est-ce que vous avez...?

## ▶Notes

_____

_____

_____

_____

_____

_____

_____

between the airport and Denfert-Rochereau Métro station every 15-20 minutes and costs €7. The buses run daily from 6am-11:30pm and take approximately 30 minutes.

## ▸Coach

Eurolines buses arrive and depart from **Gare Routière Eurolines** in Bagnolet. To get there, take the Métro to Gallini.

## ▸Rail

Paris has six train stations that each service various destinations within France and Europe. The Eurostar, (Paris-London), arrives and departs from **Gare du Nord**.

## ▸Getting Around

The public transport system, **RATP**, is comprised of buses, trams, suburban trains (RER) and the Métro (subway). RATP tickets are used interchangeably on the bus, Métro and RER. Ticket prices vary depending on the zones to which you are traveling (the city center is in zones 1 and 2). A single fare is €1.70 or you can save money by purchasing a ten-pack or "carnet" for €12.70. Free maps are available at any Métro station.

The **Métro** is the cheapest and best way to get around Paris. You can use a travel pass (below) or purchase a ticket at the station. Métro tickets must be validated before boarding. The Métro operates from 5:20am-1:20am (2:20am Saturday nights). www.parismetro.com

The **RER** express trains run underground through the city center into the surrounding suburbs, including to the Versailles region. You can use a travel pass (below) or purchase a ticket at the station. Each RER station requires your ticket in order for you to leave the station. Trains run daily from 4:45am - 1:30am. www.ratp.fr

**Buses** run daily from 5:30am – 8:30pm. You can use a travel pass or purchase a ticket on the bus. If you are traveling late at night, you will need to catch the **Noctilien** (12:30am - 5:30am), which costs €1.70 or use the Carte Orange or Paris Visite pass.

### Ⓢ Paris Visite Pass

This visitor pass allows you unlimited travel on the entire RATP network for 1, 2, 3 or 5 days and for zones 1-3, and 1-6. Fares range from €9.75 (1-day, zone 1-3) to €53.40 (5-day, zone 1-6). It also gives you discounts at various tours, attractions, museums and restaurants. Purchase at main Métro, RER stations and tourist offices. Find the English tourist page on www.ratp.fr.

## ▸Featured Hostels

See **page 111** for a key to hostel icons

### ST CHRISTOPHER'S INN PARIS
159 rue de Crimée
Dorms €15+; T: Laumiere Metro station/ Crimée train Station. (140-343-440)
www.st-christophers.co.uk/paris
*Brand new purpose built Hostel in Paris just 2 stops on the Metro. The most modern Backpackers Hostel in Paris with the best tours, packages and facilities. Live music, a great Belushi's Bar, free internet and the backdrop used in the fantastic film Amélie.*

## ▸Add'l Hostels

**Aloha Hostel**
1, rue Borromee, *near Champs-elysee*
M: Volontaires (01-42-73-03-03)

**Auberge Int'l des Jeunes**
10, Rue Trousseau, *City Centre*
M: Ledru Rollin (01-47-00-62-00)

**Blue Planet**
05 rue Hector Malot, *City Centre*
M: Gare de Lyon (01-43-42-06-18)

**3 Ducks Hostel**
6 pl. Etienne Pernet, *near Eiffel Tower*.
M: Commerce (01-48-42-04-05)

**Auberge Jules Ferry (YHA)**
8 Blvd. Jules Ferry, *Gare du L'est*
M: Republique (01-43-57-55-60)

**Young and Happy Hostel**
80 rue Mouffetardt, *Latin Quarter*
M: Place Monge (01-45-35-09-53)

**Le Village Hostel**
20 rue d'Orsel, *Montmarte*
M: Anvers (01-42-64-22-02)

**Woodstock Hostel**
48 rue Rodier, *Montmarte*
M: Poissonniere (01-48-78-87-76)

**Friend's Hostel**
122 Boulevard de la Chapelle
M: Barbès-Rochechouart
(01-42-23-45-64)

## ▸▸Things to See & Do

### ▸▸Tourist Information
Office de Tourism de Paris is located at 127 Champs-Elysées and is open daily 9am – 8pm. (01-49-52-53-54). Smaller offices are located at train station Gare de Lyon and at the Tour Eiffel (May – Sept.). Pick up a copy of the *Paris Free Voice* for local happenings in English.

### Left Bank/Right Bank
The Paris city center is split by the **River Seine** into the Left Bank and Right Bank. Below is a list of attractions by bank location. Further information about most of these attractions follows.

*Left Bank* - Îl de la Cité, Notre Dame, Ste Chapel, Conciergerie, Île St Louis, Latin Quarter, Panthéon, Sorbonne, Jardin du Luxembourg, Catacombes, Musée d'Orsay, Musée Rodin, Tombeau de Napolean, Eiffel Tower.

*Right Bank* – Jardin du Trocadéro, Louvre, Place Vendôme, Musée de l'Orangerie, Place de la Concorde, Champs-Élysées, Arc de Triomphe, Centre Georges Pompidou (Musée National d'Arte Moderne), Les Halles, The Marais, Place des Vosges, Musée Picasso, Bastille, Opéra Garnier, Montmartre, Place du Tertre, Pigalle, Cimetière du Père Lachaise.

### ▸▸Tours
#### ⑤ Balabus
The Balabus bus route from Gare de Lyon to Granse Arche de la Defense takes in many of Paris' major sights. Running daily, every 20 minutes, from 12pm to 9pm, April to Sept. It costs a single bus fare or you can use one of the many visitor passes.

### ▸▸Museums
#### ⑤ Musée Picasso *(Right Bank)*
The museum which contained over 3000 works of art by Pablo Picasso, including drawings, ceramics and paintings and which was complemented by Picasso's own personal art collection including works by Cézanne and Matisse. The museum is closed for renovations until summer 2013. 5, rue de Thorigny. M: Saint Paul. www.musee-picasso.fr

#### ⑤ Museum/Monument Pass
Get unlimited access to 60 museums and monuments for 2 (€39), 4 (€54) and 6 (€69) days. Available at all Métro stations and tourist offices. en.parismuseumpass.com

#### Ⓕ Musée du Louvre *(Left Bank)*
One of the world's largest and most exceptional museums, it houses the Mona Lisa among many other magnificent works of art. Located at the bot-

▸▸Notes

tom of the Champs-Elysées, the Louvre is open daily (except Tuesday) from 9am to 6pm (9:45pm on Wed/Fri). Admission is €11-15 and is **free** on the first Sunday of each month for all visitors and Fridays from 6pm for visitors under age 26. M: to Palais-Royal - Musée du Louvre. www.louvre.fr

### Ⓕ Musée Rodin *(Left Bank)*
The talented French sculptor's masterpieces are housed in this charming museum and garden on 79 rue Verenne. Admission is €10.80 (reduced rate €5). Garden only costs €1. Free first Sunday of each month. Closed Mondays. M: Varenne. www.musee-rodin.fr

### Ⓕ Musée d'Orsay *(Left Bank)*
Splendid collection of artwork by greats such as Cezanne, Gaugin, Monet and Manet (1848 – 1914) displayed in a beautifully renovated train station. Open daily except Monday. Admission is €9 or €6.50 after 4:30pm (6pm Thurs). Free first Sunday of each month. 1 rue de Bellechasse. M: Solferinl www.musee-orsay.fr

### Ⓕ Centre Georges Pompidou *(Right Bank)*
One of the most popular museums in Paris, this impressive centre houses works of art of the twentieth century, from late Impressionists to modern artists such as Kandinsky and Warhol (4th floor - Musée National d'Arte Moderne).

Be sure to check out the high-tech Bibliotèque Publique d'Information on the 2nd floor. The ultra modern building is open daily except Tuesday, 11am to 9pm, costs from €13 (€10 for ages 18-25). Free first Sunday of month. M: Rambuteau or Châlet-Les Halles. www.centrepompidou.fr

### ▶Neighborhoods
### Montmartre *(Right Bank)*
Once home to Picasso and Salvador Dali, this heavily touristed, yet still romantic neighborhood, is full of quaint little streets and shops. Whether you go there to visit the nearby **Sacré-Coeur** or just to sit in one of the many cafés and people watch, it's worth a look. M: Lamarck Caul/Abbesses

### Pigaille *(Right Bank)*
Known for its sleazy cabarets (Moulin Rouge), Pigaille is full of activity and energy that draws tourists to its many night clubs, bars and cafés.

### The Marais *(Right Bank)*
More sophisticated than the Pigaille or Montmarte, this charming neighborhood attracts visitors to its stylish boutiques, art galleries, cafés and the beautifully carved doors on its many historical buildings. East of Roman rue St-Martin and rue du Renard. M: Châtelet.

### ▶Notes

### Latin Quarter (Left Bank)

Artsy and academic, the Latin Quarter is filled with Paris's young, liberal students. The beautiful medieval streets lined with cafés and stylish shops are increasingly touristy, yet still charming and inviting. M: St. Michele.

### Avenue des Champs-Elysées (Right Bank)

One of Paris's most famous avenues, this thoroughfare sits amidst the Place de la Concorde and l'Arc de Triomphe. It's not exactly relaxing or even charming, but it certainly speaks of Paris's grand historic past and thriving contemporary culture.

## ▶▶ Attractions

### Arc de Triomphe (Right Bank)

Anchored in the middle of Place Charles de Gaulle and at the end of the 12 avenues, this historical monument was commissioned by Napoleon in 1806 to honor himself. It is also the site of the tomb of the unknown soldier where a flame is lit each night at 6:30pm. You may climb to the top daily for €8 (€5 ages 18-25). M: Place Charles de Gaulle - Etoile. www.arcdetriompheparis.com

### Cimetière du Père Lachaise

One of the most visited cemeteries in the world. The tombs of **Jim Morrison** and Oscar Wilde, among other notables, are here. M: Père Lachaise. www.pere-lachaise.com

### Les Catacombes

Back in 1785, the Parisian government solved the overflowing cemetery problem by removing buried bones of over 6 million people and placing them in underground quarries. Today you can walk 20 meters under the ground and view these remains. Open Tues-Sun from 10pm -5pm. Costs €8 or €6 for youth aged 14-26. 1 Place Denfert-Rochereau. M: Denfert-Rochereau. www.catacombes-de-paris.fr

### ⒻSacré-Coeur (Right Bank)

Visit this beautiful white-domed structure to take in one of the most breathtaking views of the city. Open daily, 9am to 5:45pm. Free. Located at 35 rue du Chevalier-de-la-Barre. M: Abbesses or Anvers. www.sacre-coeur-montmartre.com

### ⒻLa Samaritaine Rooftop

Excellent and free views of Paris are had from the rooftop of this department store at 142, rue de Rivoli. M: Pont Neuf.

### ⒻJardin Du Trocadéro
(Right Bank)

Stroll through these beautiful gardens while taking in renowned sculptures and visiting one of two museums, Musée de l'Homme and Musée de la Maritime. M: Trocadéro.

▶▶ Notes

_____
_____
_____
_____
_____
_____
_____
_____
_____
_____
_____
_____
_____
_____
_____
_____
_____
_____
_____
_____
_____
_____
_____
_____
_____
_____
_____
_____

# ⟫Spain

PORTUGAL

SPAIN

FRANCE

Paris ★

La Coruna · El Ferrol
Pontevedra · Oviedo
Santander ·
Porto · Bilbao
Zamora · Valladolid
Salamanca ·
Zaragoza ·
Lisbon ★
Toledo · **Madrid** ★
Barcelona
Lagos · Cordoba · Valencia
Seville ·
Cadiz · Malaga · Murcia
Gibraltar
Tetouan
Rabat ★ Algiers ★
Casablanca

*Mediterranean Sea*

ALGERIA

MOROCCO

| 0 | 210 | 420 Miles |

| 0 | 210 | 420 KM |

## ▶▶Madrid

Madrid is somewhat daunting and not so pretty at first, but after a couple of days in this bustling city, you will understand why it is the capital of Spain. Large and vibrant with an equally energetic population, Madrid's cafés, bars and nightclubs are never-ending…it's almost exhausting. There are a number of parks, monuments and museums, including the must-see **Prado**, to occupy your days. Take your time and explore the cities restaurants, shops, markets and historic sites…including taking in a bullfight (Sundays and holidays). **To See/Do**: Prado, Plaza de Toros bullfight, Palacio Real, Puerta de Sol.

### ▶▶SALAMANCA

Known for its large university and student population, Salamanca is a pillar in the Castilian region. Sitting between Madrid and Portugal, it is one of the most beautiful cities in Spain. Golden standstone buildings sit amidst grand Gothic, Renaissance and Baroque architecture. Glorious plazas, such as the incomparable Plaza Mayor, unfold unique bazaars and shops. Boasting some of the most exceptional cathedrals and churches, this historic city is easily explored on foot. **To See/Do**: Casa de la Conchas, Catedral Nueva, Catedral Vieja, Plaza Mayor.

### ▶▶SEVILLA

The essence of Moorish Spain, historic Sevilla is a crucial stop if you plan on exploring Spain. There is so much to learn, see and do in this city of Carmen, Figaro and Don Juan. Sitting on the banks of the Rio Guadalquivir, Sevilla's beauty shines not just in its many churches, balconies, bull rings and gothic architecture, but in the warm, sensual charm and wit of Sevillians themselves. **To See/Do**: Cathedral & Giralda Tower, Alcazar, Santa Cruz quarter, Triana quarter, La Maestranza bullring.

### ▶▶COSTA DEL SOL

Extending from Malaga towards Gibraltar, with towns such as Torremolinos and Marbella in between, the Costa del Sol is a great departure from the provincial and historical character of much of Andalucia. High rise hotels, packed beaches, jammed nightclubs, and lots of flashy jewelry, clothes and cars give off a Miami Beach feel (towns towards Almeria, such as Nerja, have prettier beaches and more character).

### ▶▶GRANADA

Most flock to this historic Andalucian city for a glimpse of the magnificent Alhambra. Sitting in the shadow of the stunning Sierra Nevada mountains, this city still has a haunting Moorish flavor and a mystical feeling. **To See/Do**: Alhambra, Albaicín (Old Arab Quarter), Plaza Nueva.

## ▶Visitor Info

www.tourspain.es
www.okspain.org (visa)

## ▶▶Quick Facts

**Calling Information**
*Country Code*: 34

*Calling in Spain*:
add a "0" before the area code

*Calling overseas*: 00+country code+area code+number

**Currency & Exchange Rates**
*Currency*: Euro (€)

*Exchange Rates*: €1 costs: US$1.30/ £.81/AUD$1.24/ CAN$1.28

## ▶▶Featured Hostels

See **page 111** for a key to hostel icons

### EQUITY POINT GIRONA

Plaça Catalunya 23, *Girona*
Dorms €17+; Private: €90+.
(97-241-7840)
www.equity-point.com
*Located in the best area of Girona close to all main areas of the city we offer 2,3 4, 5 and 6 bed dorm ensuites. Equity Point offers two big common areas with free wi-fi and also spectacular terrace views.*

### EQUITY POINT MADRID

C/Cruz 5, *Madrid*
Dorms €15+; Private: €30+/pp.
(915-323-122)
www.equity-point.com
*In a prime location just minutes from the Puerta del Sol. With more than 100 ensuite rooms, the hostel offers twins/doubles for privacy and dorms for an unbeatable price.*

### CAT'S HOSTEL

Cañizares 6
Dorms €15+;(44-208-600-7518)
www.famoushostels.com/madrid-hostel
*Cat's Hostel is the new youth hostel in Madrid, designed for you. We know exactly how to please our guests with a clean, comfortable and central place, in a fun area, with excellent nightlife.*

# ▶Barcelona

**BARCELONA,** delightfully eccentric, enthusiastically modern and tirelessly festive, is an essential stop on any European tour. Reborn since the demise of Spanish dictator, Franco, Barcelona's development was spurred when it hosted the 1992 Olympics. Since then, it has regained a spot as one of Europe's most beautiful, interesting and cutting-edge cities.

## ▶Getting There

By rail Barcelona is 10-12 hours south of Paris, 12.5 hours south west of Milan, 12.5 hours southwest of Zürich and 6 hours east of Madrid.

### ▶From the Airport

Barcelona's sleek international airport, **El Prat de Llobregat,** lies just outside the city center. RENFE, the Spanish national rail system, operates train service from the airport to two stops: Plaça Catalunya and Estació Sants. It costs €2.20 and takes 25 minutes. The **Aerobus** (www.aerobusbcn.com) is closer to the terminals and runs approximately every 5-20 minutes until 1am, costs €5.75 one way, €9.95 return, and takes 35 minutes.

### ▶Rail

Barcelona is a major rail center with trains arriving from throughout Spain and internationally (via France). The two main stations are **Estació Sants** and **Estació de França.** Estació Sants, located on Plaça dels Països Catalans (metro L3: Sants Estació) is the larger of the two, handling almost all service within Spain and some trains from France. Estació França handles the bulk of the international service. It is located on Avinguda del Marqués de 1'Argentera (metro L4: Barceloneta). Both stations have baggage lockers for your convenience.

The main travel information and reservation center is in Estació Sants. However, tickets can be booked at both major stations and the Passeig de Gracia station.

### ▶Bus

The main bus station is **Estació del Nord**, located 1.5 blocks from the Arc de Triomf metro stop (L1). Some buses, including those internationally bound, leave from Estació d'Autobusos de Sants, located behind Estació Sants train station.

## ▶Getting Around

Due in part to hosting the '92 Olympics, Barcelona has a fantastic transit system with fast, air-condi-

### ▶Visitor Info

www.barcelonaturisme.com

See page 102 for a Barcelona city map

### ▶Quick Facts

**Calling Information**

*Country Code*: 34

*Calling in Spain*: add a "0" before the area code

*Calling overseas*: 00+country code+area code+number

**Currency & Exchange Rates**

*Currency*: Euro (€)

*Currency Breakdown*:
100 cents=1 €

*Exchange Rates*: €1 costs: US$1.30/ £.81/AUD$1.24/ CAN$1.28

**Must See/Must Do**

La Rambla ,Chorizo, Football!

**Say What!**

Where is=Dónde está...?; How much is it=Cuánto cuesta?; Do you speak English=Habla inglés? I'd like=Quisiera

tioned cars that zip along the city's five metro lines. Tickets can be purchased inside every metro station. **Metro** hours are Mon-Thur and Sun, 5am-12am, Fri-Sat, 5am-2am. After 12am yellow night buses (all of which pass through Plaça de Catalunya) pick up the slack.

Regular metro and bus fare options include a single trip for €2, the **T-10 card** which is valid for 10 trips for €9.45, the **T-Dia card** which is an unlimited day card from €7 Zone 1 to €19.60 Zone 1-6.

Alternatively, the Tourist Card includes unlimited travel on the metro, bus, urban line, TRAM and Renfre for €13 (2-days) up to €28.50 (5-days). www.tmb.cat

## ▶Things to See & Do

### ▶Tourist Information

The Centre d'Informació Turisme de Barcelona is located underground at Plaça de Catalunya 17. It is open daily, 8:30am to 8:30pm (M: Catalunya). Two smaller offices are located at Estació Sants and at the airport.

### ▶Attractions

### Las Ramblas

A nearly two-mile long, tree-lined pedestrian thoroughfare – it's the city's most famous and active section. People from all over the world congregate at the numerous outdoor cafés and public benches to meet, greet, people watch and enjoy impressive street performances. Walking from **Plaça de Catalunya** to the **Mediterranean**, you will find vendors selling all sorts of crafts, artists displaying their works, and the colorful **Mercat de la Bouqueria** (food market – a great place to shop for a meal: olives, cheese, jamon and bread!).

At night, Las Ramblas is equally as entertaining, especially within the many gorgeous plazas that are framed by stunning romantic architecture and traditional fountains. Check out **Plaça Reial** for its many bars, outdoor cafés and clubs make for a great night's adventure.

### Barri Gòtic

Sprawling to the east of Las Ramblas is the historic and hauntingly beautiful Barri Gòtic. Barcelona's medieval center is a maze of dark narrow streets encased by endless medieval structures, including churches, courtyards and plazas. Immerse yourself in the intense character and history of these gothic and mysterious surroundings while shopping at the many eccentric curiosity shops, flea markets and craft artisans.

A particularly interesting and lively spot includes the **Plaça de Sant Josep Oriol** (plaza with arts and

## ▶Featured Hostels

See **page 111** for a key to hostel icons.

### EQUITY POINT GOTHIC

Vigatans 5, *City Center*
Dorms €17+; M: Line 4 (yellow)
to Jaume I (93-231-2045)
www.equity-point.com
*Equity Point Gothic is a lively hostel in the very centre of the city. We are located just 150 metres from the Picasso Museum. Only 2 minutes walking to Las Ramblas.*

### EQUITY POINT CENTRIC

Passeig De Gracia.
Dorms €14+, Private €48+;
M: Passeig de Gracia (93-231-2045)
www.equity-point.com
*Impressive modernist building completely refurbished in the best location ever dreamed for a hostel. More than 400 beds next to Catalunya Sq. and las Ramblas. Totally focused to the international traveller.*

### BE SOUND HOSTEL

C/ Nou de la Rambla 91
Dorms €12+. M: L2,L3 Paral.lel
(93-185-0800)
http://behostels.com/sound
*Enjoy your Barcelona experience to the extreme staying at the most original and cheap hostel: Be Sound Hostel Barcelona*

### EQUITY POINT SEA

Plaza del Mar 1-4.
Dorms €16+; M: Barceloneta.
(93-231-2045)
www.equity-point.com
*A lively hostel located in front of the most popular beach in Barcelona and only 10 minutes walking to Las Ramblas and the City Center. Have a a beer in our lobby bar and enjoy the magnificent sea views.*

crafts, musicians and cafés), **Calle de Ferran**, and the streets surrounding the church **Santa Maria del Mar**.

## Passeig de Gràcia/L'Eixample

An interesting, lively neighborhood with many students and relaxing cafés. Set in the middle of the area of **L'Eixample**, **Passeig de Gracia** offers a great view into Barcelona life minus all the tourists. Catalan is the native language of these streets. M: Passeig de Gràcia.

Don't miss the exquisite architecture found throughout the l'Eixample neighborhood, particularly on Passeig de Grácia, Rambla de Catalunya and the streets that pass between them. Of note are Antoni Gaudi's **Casa Batlló** and **La Pedrera** (Passieg de Gracia nos. 43 & 92).

## La Sagrada Familia/Antoni Gaudi

Antoni Gaudi was at the forefront of modernismé, a period in which Catalan national culture flourished and Catalan identity was cultivated through the arts, most of all architecture. Gaudi's tiled, curving, seemingly melting buildings are unlike any other architect's work. One of the most impressive is the beautiful La Sagrada Familia. A masterpiece of 8 towers, you can enter the towers for an admission fee of €13. Open daily from 9am to 6pm (8pm Apr-Sept) M: Sagrada Familia. www.sagradafamilia.org

## Ⓕ Montjuïc/Olympic Remnants

Montjuïc is a hill to the west of Las Ramblas that overlooks the city. Situated on the hill is a beautiful castle, many museums, the "Olympic Ring" and various sports facilities that supported the events. Viewing many of these sites make for great, free sightseeing as entry to the Olympic Stadium is free. Also visit the fun and interesting **Poblo Espanyol** where by day you can buy little trinkets from the many craft vendors and by night enjoy the bustling bars and cafés.

## Seaport/Barceloneta

Another area that saw much redevelopment for the Olympics was the port or waterfront at the bottom of Las Ramblas known as **La Barceloneta**. With many nightclubs, restaurants and shops, this is a great place to view modern public sculpture including the most famous, **Fish**, by American architect Frank Gehry. Beware of pickpockets at night in this area.

## Ⓕ Museu Picasso

Focusing on Picasso's earlier years, it is the most impressive Picasso collection in Spain, and is housed in beautiful medieval surroundings. Open Tues to Sun, 10am-8pm. Admission is €11. Free first Sunday of each month and every Sunday after 3pm. Carrer de Montcada 15-19. M: Jaume. www.museupicasso.bcn.es

Paris
FRANCE

Zurich
SWITZ.

Vienna
AUSTRIA

Ljubljana
SLOVENIA

Turin
Venice
Genoa
Ravenna
San Marino
Florence
Ancona
Mediterranean
Sea
Piombino
Perugia
Ajaccio
Corsica
Rome
ITALY
Sassari
Siniscola
Naples
Bari
Oristano
Sardinia
Taranto
Carbonia
Lanusei
Cetraro
Cagliari
Amantea
Crotone
Palermo

0          210          420 Miles

0     210     420 KM

## ▶Amalfi Coast

If you've ever wondered where the Italy of imposing cliffs, quaint white villages with flowering baskets and colorful little boats docked in blue azure waters are, then head to the Amalfi coast. This picture-perfect setting is situated just south of Naples, overlooking the Bay of Salerno. The only disappointments may be the heavy throngs of vacationers in the summer months and corresponding high prices. Go for a day or two, though, and stay in the more tame and affordable Amalfi, as Positano tends to host only the very wealthy.

## ▶Venice

Regardless of the hordes of tourists and the higher than normal prices (relative to Italy) of this enchanting city, words or images cannot prepare you for the unique and unforgettable experience Venice offers. Whether you indulge in culture and art, history, romance and nightlife, it will be tainted with an intriguing, enduring and exotic flavor that cannot properly be described. By foot and gondola you can explore glorious landmarks, romantic canals and exciting markets. **To See/Do**: Check the tourist office for possible free tours, Basilica di San Marco (strict dress code), Palazzo Ducale, Piazza San Marco, Campanile.

## ▶Milan

Milan, although a historic city with centuries of war and dynastic influence, is today mainly a modern commercial hub and is best suited as a quick stopover on the way to somewhere more inspiring and interesting. For a day or so, though, it's worth exploring the city's ancient churches, monuments and museums as well as browsing through the countless shops and cafés. As the center of international fashion and style, Milan has a cutting edge cosmopolitan flair, attested to by its hip bars, nightclubs and cafés. At the tourist office, pick up a copy of the free city entertainment guide, *Milano Mese*, for the latest happenings. **To See/Do**: Duomo, Castello Sforzesco (fortress), Pinacoteca (museum).

## ▶Naples/Pompeii/Capri

Quintessentially Italian in all stereotypes...imageries, personalities, geographically. The intensity of the heavily populated city of Naples is at once captivating and complicated. Lying on the south eastern Italian coastline at the bottom of the imposing Mt. Vesuvius, it is busy, loud, dirty and known for much mafia-related crime (petty crime is also high, so watch your wallet and money belt). Amidst this madness, though, you are treated to fiery Italian personalities, preparing some of the most authentic pizza and pasta dishes in Italy and adhering to genuine southern Italian traditions. Added bonuses to this

## ▶Visitor Info

www.italiantourism.com

## ▶▶Quick Facts

**Calling Information**
*Country Code*: 39

*Calling in Italy*: add a "0" before the area code

**Currency & Exchange Rates**
*Currency*: Euro (€); 100 cents=1 €

*Exchange Rates*: €1 costs: US$1.30/ £.81/AUD$1.24/ CAN$1.28

## ▶▶Highlights

Venice, Spanish Steps, Amalfi Coast, Florence.

## ▶▶Italy Hostels

### ▶▶Amalfi Coast
**Hostel Brikette**
Via G Marconi 358, *Positano*
(089-875-857)

**A Scalinatella Hostel**
Piazza Umberto 1, n 5/6, *Amalfi Coast*. (089-871-492)

### ▶▶Venice
**Archie's House**
San Leonardo 1814 B
(041-720-884)

**Camping Alba D'Oro**
Via Triestina 10, *Ca' Noghera*
(041-541-5102)

**Camping Fusina**
Via Moranzani 79
(041-547-0055)

**Plus Alba D'Oro Hostel**
Via Triestina, 214G, *Venice*
(041-541-5102)

**Plus Jolly Campsite**
Via G. de Marchi 7, Marghera, *Venice* (041-920-312)

**Venezia Youth Hostel (HI)**
Fondamenta Zitelle 86, *Giudecca*
(041-523-8211)

### ▶▶Milan
**Piero Rotta Youth Hostel**
Via Martino Bassi 2
(023-926-7095)

already hyped scene are the nearby sites of ancient **Pompeii** and **Herculaneum** and the beautiful island of **Capri**. Pompeii and Herculaneum, about half an hour from Naples city, are the extremely well preserved sites of ancient Rome. Tour the fascinating remains of the old Roman town, including villas, official buildings and theaters. The picturesque Capri, an excellent day trip, is accessed by ferries from Naples (little over an hour trip). Beautiful cliffs, little villages and blue waters await. It's not cheap, though, and is insanely crowded in the summer, but certainly worth a day and a night.

## ▶Cinque Terre

On the Northeast coast of Italy, the impressive Five Villages are a delight to any traveler. Situated between Genoa and La Spezia, these stunning villages envelop you in golden sandy beaches, steep cliffs and sapphire-colored water. Although these days the region is certainly known to many travelers, each town is still very cozy and offers a quiet haven from the big city tourism encountered in Florence or Venice. Sleep late, sit on the beach, go hiking or have a picnic. The five towns (north to south): Monterosso al Mare, Vernazza, Corniglia, Manarola, Riomaggiore.

## ▶Tuscany

No trip to Florence is complete without a visit to the captivating nearby region of Tuscany. Famous for its golden sunsets, stunning landscapes and enchanting wineries, the hills and towns of Tuscany are a traveler's delight. Stroll through narrow winding streets, explore ancient architecture, indulge in delicious Etruscan cuisine and sample some of the best wines in the world. The region is easily visited via bus from Florence. Buses have specific destinations or towns – check with the tourist info center. Or better yet, rent a car and explore the region on your own. Certain towns are best explored on foot, in which case you can just park the car at the city gates. Listed below are just some of the delightful towns to check out:

*Chianti* - famous for its rolling vineyards and delicious vintages. The picture perfect vineyards are open to the public where you may walk through fields of sunflowers, wildflowers and rambling vines. *San Gimignano* – known for its far reaching stone towers that create a unique and stunning skyline. Its narrow streets and gorgeous piazzas are captivating. *Cortona* – often the backdrop in many writings, this medieval town has a sort of quirky charm that intrigues visitors from all over the world. In fact, its unique character has attracted a sizeable community of foreign residents. *Lucca* – Rich in historic architecture, Lucca (close to Pisa) charms you with little shops, restaurants and remarkable churches. *Montepulciano* – with a maze of narrow streets, medieval and Renaissance architecture and famous vineyards, it is a must see.

## ▶Hostels Con't

### ▶Naples, Pompeii & Capri

**Hostel of the Sun**
Via Melisurgo 15, *Naples*
(081-420-6303)

**Hostel & Hotel Bella Capri**
Via Melisurgo 4, *Naples*
(081-552-9494)

**Mergellina Youth Hostel**
Salita della Grotta a Piedigrotta 23, *Naples* (081-761-2346)

**Hostel of the Sun/Bella Capri**
Via Melisurgo 15, *Naples*
(081-420-6393)

**Casa del Pellegrino Youth Hostel**
Via Duca d'Aosta, *Pompeii*
(081-761-2346)

### ▶Cinque Terre

**Ostello Cinque Terre**
via Riccobaldi 21, *Manarola*
(0187-920-215)

# ▸▸Florence

FLORENCE, once the center of Renaissance art and culture, today remains an intriguing and alluring city. Although inundated with tourists, you can still immerse yourself in its rich history and Italian culture. Don't miss the surrounding golden countryside which tempts you with the promise of a true Tuscan experience.

## ▸▸Getting There

### ▸▸From the Airport

**Amerigo Vespucci Airport** or **Peretola** is located about 30 minutes away from downtown Florence. VolainBus Airport Shuttle (www.ataf.net) costs €6 and heads to Florence City Center/Central Station. You can also fly to nearby **Galileo Galilei Airport** in Pisa, where there is direct rail service into Florence (takes 1 hour).

### ▸▸Rail

The main train station, **Santa Maria Novella**, is a 5 minute walk from the Duomo and the city center.

### ▸▸Bus

The main bus station is located right across the street from the train station. From here, SITA operates an extensive route of buses to the Tuscan countryside, the only affordable way to see this magnificent landscape.

## ▸▸Getting Around

The best and easiest way to get around Florence is on foot. There are public buses that run throughout the city. Tickets cost €1.20 (70 minutes), €5(24 hrs) and €12(3 days) . Tickets are not sold on the bus, but at newsstands and tobacco shops. www.ataf.net

## ▸▸Things to See & Do

### ▸▸Tourist Information

The main tourist information center is north of the Duomo at Via Cavour 1r (055-290-832 or 055-290-833). Hours of operation are Mon to Sat, 8:30am to 6:30pm (Sundays until 1:30pm). Another tourist center is located across the street from Stazione di Santa Maria Novella at Piazza della Stazione 4. It is open Mon to Sat, 8:30am to 7pm (Sundays until 2:00pm). The third center, which is usually less crowded, is located at Borga Santa Croce 29r. Open daily from 9am to 7pm (Sundays until 2pm).

### ▸▸Sights & Attractions
#### Ⓕ Il Duomo

The most famous building in Florence is probably Il Duomo, or the cathedral. Located in the heart of the old city, this massive church is made of the

## ▸▸Web Links

**Visitor Information**
www.turismo.toscana.it

## ▸▸Quick Facts

**Calling Information**
*Country Code*: 39

*Calling in Italy*: add a "0" before the area code

*Calling overseas*: 00+country code+area code+number

**Currency & Exchange Rates**
*Currency*: Euro (€)

*Currency Breakdown*:
100 cents =1 €

*Exchange Rates*: €1 costs: US$1.30/ £.81/AUD$1.24/ CAN$1.28

**Must See/Must Do**
Gelato, Outdoor Markets, Duomo Tower, Tuscan Countryside

**Say What!**
Where is =Dov´è...?; How much is it=Quanto costa?; Do you speak English=Parla inglese?; I'd like = Vorrei...; Do you have=Ha delle...?

## ▸▸Notes

_____

_____

_____

_____

_____

_____

_____

beautiful green, white, and red marble that distinguishes the outstanding and unique buildings of Tuscany. Built by Bruneslleschi at the beginning of the Renaissance, the dome was then the largest in the world. www.duomofirenze.it

(F) Il Duomo is open Mon to Fri, 10am to 5pm, Sun 1:30pm to 4:45pm (free admission). Should you challenge yourself and climb all the way to the top of the dome, you'll be treated to a stunning view of the city of Florence and its countryside. The Dome is open Mon to Fri, 8:30am to 7:00pm, Sat 8:30am to 5:40pm and is closed on Sundays. Dome admission is €8.

## Ponte Vecchio
This pedestrian bridge across the Arno River might well be the city's emblem. Once the home of the city's meatpackers, it was when the Medici family decided that the river was made unattractive from all the blood from the cut up poultry that the meatpackers were replaced with gold jewelers. Today the jewelers remain among the markets and touristy shops.

## (F) Boboli Gardens
On the west side of the Arno River are the Boboli Gardens, a wonderful respite from Florence's dark and narrow streets. One can spend hours exploring the well-manicured paths and beautiful fountains. There are also fantastic views of the city.

## ▸▸Museums
The museums in Florence are exceptional and a must see. Florence was the center of the Renaissance, and accordingly, has the most famous works from this period displayed in various halls around the city.

## Galleria dell' Academia
Host to several brilliant Renaissance works of art, including the famous **Michelangelo's David**, this museum is a must just for a peek at the star attraction. Via Ricasoli 60. Open Mon 8:15am-2pm; Tue-Sun 8:15am to 7:15pm. Costs €14. www.gallerieaccademia.org

## Uffizi Gallery
The most famous gallery in Florence, it houses masterpieces from all the Italian greats such as **Michelangelo, da Vinci, Raphael** and **Botticellis**. Brave the lines, as you shouldn't need more than a couple of hours once inside. You can also avoid lines by making a reservation in advance with the museum office for €3 extra. Open Tues to Sun, 8:30am to 7pm (closed on Mondays). Costs €9.50. www.uffizi.com

## ▸▸Shopping
Known for its leather goods, wool garments and jewelry, Florence's markets and shops are a great place to find terrific bargains. Check out the areas of **San Lorenzo**, near the Mercato Centrale, and the **Ponte Vecchio**.

## ▸▸Florence Hostels

**Bigallo Youth Hostel**
V. Bigallo e Apparita 14
(055-630-907)

**Europa-Villa Camerata YH**
Viale Augusto Righi 4
(055-601-451)

**Villa Camerata (HI)**
Viale Augusto Righi, 4
(055-601-451)

**Ostello Santa Monaca**
Via Santa Monaca 6.
(055-268-338)

**Plus Florence Hostel**
Via Santa Caterina D'Alessandria 15
(055-462-8934)

**Plus Michelangelo Campsite**
Viale Michelangelo 80.
(055-68-11-977)

**7 Santi Hostel**
Viale dei Mille, 11.
(055-504-8452)

**Hostel Camping Village Il Poggetto**
Via Il Poggetto, 143, Troghi
(055-830-7323)

# ▸▸Rome

ROME is magnificent! Nearly all of the political and cultural institutions and customs of the Western World originated here. Today, Rome struggles mightily to cope with this immensely impressive past and the current demands of modernization; subway lines may take years to complete because every inch is bound to uncover ruins dating back thousands of years. Often this mix of past and present is fascinating, but at other times, it adds confusion and disorganization to an already crowded city.

Nevertheless, Rome's magic is indeed alluring and enduring. It is an authentically Italian city harboring not just some of the most famous and historical sites and monuments, but terrific cafés, beautiful piazzas, vibrant personalities, and of course, excellent shopping. When visiting Rome, take the time to indulge in these smaller treasures and you'll understand why it is still one of the great capitals of Europe.

## ▸Getting There

Rome is located in central Italy, south of Florence (1.5 hrs), Milan (4.5 hrs) and Venice (4.5 hrs).

### ▸▸From the Airport

Rome is serviced by the modern and efficient **Leonardo da Vinci Int'l Airport**, also known as **Fiumicino**. The airport is connected to the city of Rome by the Leonardo Express train to Stazione Termini. It takes about 30 minutes and costs €14 o/w. It runs every 30 minutes from 6:38am-11:38pm daily. The Sabina-Fiumicino line (FR1) costs €8 o/w. www.adr.it/fiumicino

### ▸▸Rail

The Italian national rail company is **Ferrovile dello Stato** (FS). **Stazione Termini**, located on the Piazza de Cinquecento in the San Lorenzo neighborhood, is the main train terminal. It is a mecca of tourist necessities: ATM machines, internet stations, tourist information, a health clinic, public showers, luggage lockers and late night banks. Termini is easily accessible by the subway — it is the only place where both lines stop. By foot, it is about a 15 minute walk from the Centro Storico. The other large station is Tiburtina (see below).

### ▸▸Bus

Unfortunately there is no main bus station in Rome. Long-distance buses arrive outside various metro stations including Lepanto, Ponte Mammolo and Tiburtina. Eurolines buses arrive and depart from **Tiburtina**. From Stazione Termini take the Metropolitana (train) Linea B to Tiburtina.

## ▸▸Web Links

**Visitor Information**
www.turismoroma.it
See page 103 for Rome city map

## ▸▸Quick Facts

**Calling Information**
*Country Code*: 39

*Calling in Italy*: add a "0" before the area code

*Calling overseas*: 00+country code+area code+number

**Currency & Exchange Rates**
*Currency*: Euro (€)

*Currency Breakdown*:
100 cents=1 €

*Exchange Rates*: €1 costs: US$1.30/ £.81/AUD$1.24/ CAN$1.28

**Must See/Must Do**
Pantheon, Spanish Steps, Michelangelo, everywhere

**Say What!**
Where is=Dov'è...?; How much is it=Quanto costa?; Do you speak English=Parla inglese?; I'd like = Vorrei...; Do you have=Ha delle...?

## ▸▸Notes

-----------------------
-----------------------
-----------------------
-----------------------
-----------------------
-----------------------
-----------------------

## ▸Getting Around

Rome, a crowded and heavily trafficked city, is not known for its public transport. In fact, the best and practically only way to get around the city is by foot. The hectic and crowded streets of Rome do not make for great bus, taxi, or car travel either.

Should you venture onto one of the buses, subways or suburban trains, tickets cost €1.50 per 100 minutes (regardless of destination) and are interchangeable on all forms of public transport. You may purchase an all-day ticket for €6 or a weekly pass (CIS) for €24. Tickets must be purchased before boarding and can be purchased at many newsstands, tobacco shops, or at main subway or bus stations. Note, the fine for riding without a ticket is over €50 and is even enforced against "ignorant" pleading tourists, so buy a ticket before boarding. www.atac.roma.it

### Bus

Public buses are operated by the **ATAC**. Buses run from 5:30am to 11:30pm. After 11:30pm an erratic night bus system (notturno) runs until 5:30am. ATAC's info booth in the center of Piazza dei Cinquecento sells helpful transit maps and can give a list of all the bus routes.

### Metropolitana

Rome's subway consists of two lines, A and B, both of which skirt the city center, running between 5:30am and 11:30pm. Take Linea A to Ottaviano (Vatican City & St. Peter's), Spagna (Spanish Steps and Villa Borghese), Barberini (Trevi Fountain) and Stazione Termini. Linea B takes you to Colosseo, Circo Massimo, and Piramide/Ostiense. The neighborhood of Trastevere, south-west of the city center, is not serviced by the subway.

## ▸Things to See & Do

### ▸Tourist Information

The main APT tourist office (which is often less crowded) is located at Villa Parigi 5 and is open Mon-Friday between 8:15am-7:15pm and on Saturday until 1:45pm (06-488-991). The APT office in Stazione Termini is open daily 8:15am-9:00pm. The office in the airport is open daily 8am-7pm.

### ▸Tours

### Rome(ing) Tours

They offer 5 excellent English language walking tours for independent travelers and students, including the All Over Rome tour (3.5-4hrs) and the Vatican Tour (4-4.5hrs) for €22. They also offer a Dark Tour/Pub Crawl (€17). www.romeingtours.com

## ▸Featured Hostels

Hostel beds range from €15-18 for dorms and from €40 for private rooms with shared bath. See **page 111** for a key to hostel icons.

### ALESSANDRO PALACE HOSTEL

Via Vicenza 42
Dorms €19+, Private €25+/pp;
(44-208-600-7518)
www.famoushostels.com/rome-hostel
*Established in 1990, the Alessandro Palace Hostel has become one of the most popular hostels in Rome for backpackers & independent travellers. Located in a safe central area a short walk from Termini.*

## ▸Additional Hostels

**AF Pessina Youth Hostel**
Viale delle Olimpiadi 61
(06-323-6267)

**Alesandro Downtown**
Via Carlo Cattaneo 23
(06-4434-0147)

**The Beehive Hostel**
Via Marghera 8
(06-447-04553)

**Bella Roma Hostel**
Via E. Accinni 63
(06-3975-0599)

**Freedom Traveller Hostel**
Via Gaeta 25
(06-4782-3862)

**Hostel Des Artistes**
Via Villafranca 20
(06-445-4365)

**Hostel Pink Floyd**
Via Principe Amedeo
(06-39-74-52-28)

**M+J Place**
Via Solferino 9
(06-446-2802)

**Plus Roma Campsite**
Via Aurelia 831-Km 8,2
(06-6623-018)

**Yellow Hostel**
Via Palestro 44
(06-49-38-26-82)

### Hop-on Hop-off Bus Tour

One of the better deals in Rome, the 110 Open Bus takes you on an English speaking guided bus tour of 40 of Rome's best sites. Without getting off the bus the entire tour lasts just under 2 hours. Departures every 15 minutes from 8:30am to 8:30pm. Costs €20 for a 48-hour ticket. www.trambusopen.com

### ▶ Areas & Attractions

### Trastevere

A colorful neighborhood that demands to be explored! Its wonderful winding streets are lined with excellent bars, cafés and affordable restaurants. The nightlife here is one of the most hopping in Rome. Also check out the interesting flea market on Sunday mornings.

### Ⓕ The Pantheon

This impeccable structure, symbolizing the glory and culture of ancient Rome is remarkably well pre-served. Admission is free. Open Mon-Sat, 9am-6:30pm and Sundays from 9am-1pm.

### Colosseum

One of Rome's most visited sites, this grand arena wit-nessed some of the most brutal and bloody spectator events in ancient civilization. Open daily from 8:30am until one hour before sunset. Costs €12 for 2 day access (includes Roman Forum/Pallantine Hill (see below).

### Piazza di Spagna (Spanish Steps)

Since the 18th century, this gorgeous piazza has attracted the most beautiful and talented Romans and foreigners alike to share drink, music and con-versation. Home to the Spanish Steps (formerly the 18th century Spanish Embassy). A great spot to relax and enjoy the fantastic and constantly ac-tive scenery.

### Ⓕ Roman Forum/Pallantine Hill

The heart of ancient Rome, this site was once the pulse of the entire city. The Forum holds some of the most impressive remains that depict the com-plexities and grandeur of the Roman Empire – it should not be missed. Admission to the forum, Pallantine Hill and the Colosseum for 2 days is €12.

### Ⓕ St. Peter's Basilica

One of the largest churches in the world and one of Michelangelo's best contributions (the great dome), the **Basilica** is well worth a visit. Open 7am-7pm (until 6:30pm Oct-April). Weds 1pm to 6 or 7pm.

### Ⓕ Vatican Museum/Sistine Chapel

A massive collection of art housed in an equally enormous complex - one of the best collections in Europe. Check out the **Sistine Chapel** to gaze at Michelangelo's frescos, the Creation and the Last Judgment. Costs €15 and open M-Sat 9-6pm. Free/open on last Sunday of month from 9am-12:30pm.

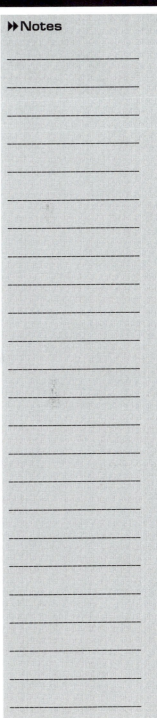

▶▶ Notes

# ▶Germany, Austria & Switzerland

DENMARK

★Copenhagen

Schleswig•

•Hamburg

Amsterdam★

NETHERLANDS

Berlin★

POLAND

BELGIUM★

•Cologne

**GERMANY**

Brussels

★Paris

•Frankfurt

★Prague

**CZECH REP.**

FRANCE

•Stuttgart

SLOVAKIA

Munich•

Vienna ★

★Bratislava

Bern

•Zurich

**AUSTRIA**

Lausanne★

**SWITZ.**

Budapest★

Geneva•

Graz•

**HUNGARY**

ITALY

Ljubljana★

Venice•

**SLOVENIA**

| 0 | 210 | 420 Miles |

| 0 | 210 | 420 KM |

## ▶Munich

Next to Berlin, this is *the* city to visit in Germany. It delightfully and authentically lives up to its status as the capital of Bavaria. This wealthy city is an emblem of German tradition and stereotype, however, Munich simultaneously embraces contemporary cutting edge culture. Their avant-garde youth scene means there's much to check out in the way of cool nightclubs, bars and restaurants. But no doubt you will inevitably (and happily) indulge in the more customary tourist scene. After exploring the many neighborhoods, museums and historical attractions, eat your fill of sausage and mustard, then wash it down with two...or three...or even four steins of beer. In fact, there are scores of beer halls, gardens and open-air markets packed with lederhosen-clad Germans drinking the day and night away listening to local oompah bands. This exciting atmosphere is so infectious that it's no mistake that Munich is the site of many festivals such as Fashing and Oktoberfest. **To See/Do:** Alte Pinakothek (art collection), Hofbräuhaus (famous beer hall), Viktualienmarkt (open-air market) and the English Garden.

## ▶Dresden

Capital of the eastern state of Saxony, Dresden is a city on the rise. The historical beauty and legacy of Dresden was disastrously bombed by the Allied forces in WWII. The tragic event, which spurred the Kurt Vonnegut novel, Slaughterhouse Five, not only destroyed beautiful and historical architecture, art and landscapes, but took the lives of tens of thousands of Germans. Post-war, many of the baroque buildings were restored, but today more than ever, the city is determined to recapture its legacy as the German "Florence" and is rebuilding many of its once glorious structures as well as encouraging tourism and cultural development. **To See/Do:** Stadtmuseum, Schloss (castle), Zwinger.

## ▶Hamburg

After Berlin and Munich, Hamburg is one of the most visited cities in Germany. Once known as "Sin City," for its notorious red light district, today it is visited for its interesting arts scene, cool bars and cafés and vibrant youth culture. Whether you indulge in its harbor and canal atmosphere (sort of like Venice) or enjoy the contrasting park-like feel throughout the city, you will thoroughly enjoy your stay. **To See/Do:** Altstadt, Kunsthalle (museum), Deichstrasse (neighborhood).

## ▶Stuttgart/Tübingen/Heidelberg

The picturesque region of Baden-Württemberg is dotted with quaint villages, university towns and of course the industrial home of Mercedes-Benz and

Calling ... ...s: 00+country code+area code+number

### Currency & Exchange Rates

Currency: Euro (€)

Exchange Rates: €1 costs: US$1.30/ £.81/AUD$1.24/ CAN$1.28

## ▶Highlights

Berlin, Köln, Romantic Road, Oktoberfest, Bavarian Forest

## ▶Featured Hostels

See **page 60** for Featured Berlin Hostels. See **page 111** for a key to hostel icons.

### FIVE ELEMENTS HOSTEL

Moselstr. 40, *Frankfurt*
Dorms €18+, Private €55+. Transport: Frankfurt Main. (069-240-05-885)
www.5elementshostel.de
*Brand new funky Backpacker Hostel in Frankfurt/Main, designed for the traveller in a completely renovated turn of the century building. Just 5 minutes walk from the main station. Spectacular skyline view!*

### SMART STAY HOSTEL MUNICH CITY

Mozartstraße 4, *Munich*
Dorms €14.90+. Transport: Main train station. (49-895-587-970)
www.smart-stay.de
*The perfect accommodation for backpackers and travel groups in Munich. The hostel is situated in the heart of the Bavarian capital, directly at the Theresienwiese, only two metro stops (10 min walk) from the city center.*

Explore the nearby university town ...km south of Stuttgart). It is a beautiful ...th lovely architecture, a great student ...ots of charm and culture. Also close by is ...erg. Idyllic in setting, complete with castles, ...ic architecture and also home to a thriving student population, Heidelberg is a traveler's delight (although too many tourists often spoil its charm). **To See/Do: Stuttgart**: Mercedes-Benz and Porsche museums; **Tübingen**: Rathaus, Schloss Hohentübingen; **Heidelberg**: Schloss, Universitätsplatz.

## **Frankfurt**

Germany's financial capital is just that...a modern, thriving business center. Largely void of old world German charm in the way of architecture, art and personality, Frankfurt is sleek, wealthy and intellectual. The city recovered from WWII by pushing towards the future and economic success rather than preserving its rather large historical legacy. It did, however, retain a few pockets of preserved culture, such as the old quarter of Sachsenhausen and is a perfect and refreshing night's stop after the medieval towns of the Romantic Road or before heading onto the less glamorous state of Saxony. **To See/Do**: Fressgasse ("Pig Out Alley"); Goethe's Museum and House; Sachsenhausen (old quarter).

## **Rothenburg/Romantic Road**

The Romantic Road is a heavily touristed route of approximately 290km between the German towns of Würzburg in the north and Füssen in the Bavarian Alps. In between are lovely medieval villages that are so picturesque it's as if they leapt out of a fairytale. You can tour the route by way of bus tours, car, rail or bicycle and stop off at each town (note: Eurail and German Rail passes can be used). There are tourist info centers along the way, but a good place to start is in either Munich or Frankfurt. Of particular interest on the route is the town of Rothenburg. It is the most visited of all the towns for its picture-perfect medieval character. As with many of the most beautiful attractions, the Romantic Road and especially Rothenburg, get absolutely mobbed with tourists, particularly in the summer months.

## **Köln**

Köln, or Cologne, is the German capital for mass media, music (nightlife), gay and lesbian life, and for its art scene. Because of Köln's central location within Europe, it is the biggest hub in Germany with direct trains to/from Amsterdam, Brussels, Paris, Zurich, Vienna, Prague and Berlin. It also serves as a new hub for the low-cost airlines with cheap fares from many cities. **To See/Do**: Koelner Dom (Cologne Cathedral).

## **Additional Hostels**

### **Köln**
**Station Hostel for Backpackers**
Marzellenstr. 44-56, *Cologne*
(0-221-912-5301)

**Youth Hostel Köln-Riehl**
An der Schanz 14
(0221-767-081)

**Youth Hostel Köln-Deutz**
Siegesstr. 5a
(0221-814-711)

### **Dresden**
**Hostel Die Boofe**
Louisenstr 20
(0351-801-3361)

**Hostel Mondpalast**
Louisenstr. 77
(0351-563-4050)

**Lollis Homestay**
Seitenstrasse 2a
(0351-799-3025)

**Youth Hostel Dresden (HI)**
Maternistr. 22
(351-49-26-20)

### **Hamburg**
**A&O City Hotel + Hostel**
Hammer Landstraße 170
(040-21-04-02-94)

**Generator Hostel**
Steinorplatz 3
(207-388-7666)

**Instant Sleep Hostel**
Max. Brauer Allee 277
(040-4318-2310)

**Schanzenstern**
Bartlestr. 12
(040-439-8441)

### **Munich**
**A&O City Hotel + Hostel**
Arnulfstraße 104.
(089-452-359-550)

**A&O City Hotel**
Bayerstraße 75.
(089-452-359-60)

### **Stuttgart**
**Stuttgart Youth Hostel**
Haußmannstr. 27
(0711-24-15-83)

# ▶▶Berlin

**BERLIN** has undergone massive reconstruction, both physically and socially, since the fall of the wall in 1989. A large influx of revolutionary, creative and bohemian people from all over Germany and the rest of Europe has created a dynamic, exciting and youthful energy. While Paris and London have traditionally served as the centers of changing European culture, attracting active and radical people from around the world, today the real modern European cultural hot-spot is Berlin. Here, the constant reminder of their difficult history in turn spawns new innovations and forethought.

Berliners think in grand terms: they see their city becoming the future center of Europe, bridging the gaps between Moscow and London, Stockholm and Rome. With a cutting-edge arts scene, terrific cafés, imaginative modern architecture and distinct and vibrant neighborhoods, it is impossible not to leave Berlin impressed, if not awestruck. Surprisingly, Berlin is far from being over-touristed. Walking the streets, you will not see crowds following umbrellas or busloads of camera-toting foreigners. Berlin should be visited for its pulsating social and cultural scene that is original, new and inspiring.

## ▶▶Getting There

By rail, Berlin is located 5 hours north of Prague, 2.5 hours southeast of Hamburg, 4 hours northeast of Frankfurt and 7-10 hours from Amsterdam.

### ▶▶From the Airport

Berlin has two airports, **Tegel** and **Schönefeld**. In March 2013, Tegel will close and Schönefeld will become the sole airport and be renamed Berlin Brandenburg International (BBI). From Tegel take **bus TXL** to Berlin Hauptbahnhof or bus X9 or 109 to Banhaff Zoo for €2.40 each way. From Schönefeld take the S9 or S45 lines.

### ▶▶Bus & Rail

The incredibly comprehensive, reliable and rapid German national rail carrier is **Deutsche Bahn** (DB). The main station is **Zoologischer Garten** (Bahnhof Zoo), located in Charlottenburg at the intersection of Hardenbergstrasse and Joachim-staler Strasse (U2, 9: Zoologischer Garten).

In the former East, station **Ostbahnhof** handles some major international and domestic routes. It is located in Friedrichshain but is only an S-Bahn station (see below). The main station is **Zentraler Omnibus-bahnhof** (ZOB) located in Charlottenburg. Take the U2 to Kaiserdamm.

▶ Berlin ▶ Th
▶Getting Aro
Berlin has one
hensive trans
subway line
train line
the BV
and
Fa

## ▶Quick Facts

### Calling Information
*Country Code*: 49

*Calling in Germany*: add a "0" before the area code

*Calling overseas*: 00+country code+area code+number

### Currency & Exchange Rates
*Currency*: Euro (€)

*Currency Breakdown*:
100 cents = 1 €

*Exchange Rates*: €1 costs: US$1.30/ £.81/AUD$1.24/ CAN$1.28

### Must See/Must Do
East Side Gallery (Berlin Wall), Club scene , Historical Walking Tour

### Say What!
Where is=Wo ist die...; How much is it=Wieviel kostet est...?; Do you speak English=Sprechen Sie Englisch?; I'd like=Ich möchte...; Do you have=Haben Sie...?

## ▶▶Notes

---

## ...und

...of the most efficient and compre-
...t systems in Europe. There are eight
...s (*U-Bahn*), along with many suburban
...s (*S-Bahn*), trams and buses operated by
...g. The city also has a terrific network of safe
...apid bike paths.

...res for the transit system are based on 3 tariff
zones: AB, BC or ABC. Most likely, unless you are
traveling further away to Potsdam, you'll only need
zones AB. Tickets for the transit system can be easily purchased from the various machines in the
U-Bahn stations.

A single ticket costs €2.40 for travel in AB tariff
zones, but you can purchase an **All-day Pass** for
€6.50 or a **7-Day Pass** for €28 (AB zones)/€34.60
(all 3 zones). Check with each station for free maps.
Note that you must validate your ticket at the
machines on the platform before boarding.
www.bvg.de

## ▶ Things to See & Do

### ▶ Tourist Information

Berlin Infostores, at the Europa-Center on Budapester
Strasse, is open Mon-Sat, 8am-10pm. Here you can
buy the *Berlin Welcome Card* (2-day €17.90, 3-day
€23.90) which gives you discounts on attractions, museums, tours and 3 days unlimited public transport.
www.visitberlin.de/en/welcomecard

Check out the book *Berlin for Young People,* sold
at many bookstores and other shops throughout
the city for about €9. It is an excellent, extensive
local guide to the neighborhood scenes.

### ▶ Tours

### Ⓢ City Bus 100

For the price of a single fare (€2.40), take bus number 100 to see many interesting sights and attractions going from Zoo Station, by the Brandenburg
Gate and Reichstag and ending in Prenzlauer Berg.
The BVG offers a brief guide giving an overview
of the tour.

### Berlin Walks

Offers excellent walks of Berlin lasting between
2-3 hours. The cost is €12 or €9 with a Berlin
Welcome Card. www.berlinwalks.de

### Brewer's Best of Berlin

Their tour is an excellent way to get acquainted
with Berlin - both its history and layout. Tours
last anywhere from 4-10 hours depending on
the day and tour guide. A great value at €15.
www.brewersberlintours.com

## ▶ Featured Hostels

See page 111 for a key to hostel
icons.

### HEART OF GOLD HOSTEL
Johannisstr. 11, *Friedrichshain*
Dorms €10+, Twin €25+;
S: Friedrichstrasse (030-29-00-33-00)
www.heartofgold-hostel.de
*The starship class in backpacking. A
state-of-the-art hostel inspired by
"The Hitchhiker's Guide to the
Galaxy." Don't Panic! All main sights
in walking distance. Vivid downtown
nightlife on the doorstep.*

### HELTER SKELTER HOSTEL
Kalkscheunenstr. 4-5, *Friedrichshain*
Dorms €10+; Twins €20+;
S: Friedrichstrasse (030-28-04-49-97)
www.helterskelterhostel.com
*The anything goes hostel. Back to the
roots of backpacking. Kitchen. No
checkout time. No rules, except: no
rudes. Get on the slide now! Most
central hostel in town. Rock n Roll! No
pets, no children, no sleeping bags.*

### ODYSSEE GLOBETROTTER HOSTEL
Gruenberger 23, *Friedrichshain*
Dorms €10+, Private €42+;
S: Ostbahnhof (030-29-00-00-81)
www.globetrotterhostel.de
*The Odyssee Globetrotter Hostel is
one of the first Hostels that opened in
Berlin in 1998! We are proud to have
maintained some original East Berlin
style and the spirit of those wild 90s
for you. Bar & restaurant, billiard, TV.*

### SUNFLOWER HOSTEL
Helsingforser Str 17, *Friedrichshain*
Dorms: €10+, Private €38+;
S: Ostbahnhof. (030-44-04-42-50)
www.sunflower-hostel.de
*One of Berlin's most popular
hostels, you gotta find out why that
is yourself. One of the reasons:
Perfectly located in the happening
and sub-cultural part of town w/
the highest concentration of clubs,
bars and restaurants.*

## ⇒ Neighborhoods

Berlin consists of extremely distinct and dynamic neighborhoods. As such, we describe the city's four most interesting and enjoyable areas below.

### Mitte

The Mitte is the historic heart of Berlin and contains many of the city's most popular tourist sites. **Unter den Linden** used to be one of the most fashionable and famous streets in Europe; today, it is mainly new embassies and fancy shops. Once across the **Spree**, however, Mitte becomes the most fashionable district in the city. Mitte was the first area of the former East to be revamped and resettled and where the whole artistic explosion first started. It was in **Tacheles** (Oranienburger Str. 53), a bombed-out Jewish department store that had been left unrepaired since the war, that the first squatters began establishing the spontaneous, erratic, and frenetic alternative arts culture that thrived immediately following the fall of the Wall. Tacheles is now preserved in its still-destructed form as an institution for contemporary art. It is a must see by day and by night: inside there are artists living and working, a fantastic café, an alternative movie theater, and a music venue.

### Prenzlauer Berg

A bohemian neighborhood, even under Communist rule, that has now become an incredible conglomerate of beautiful buildings, streets and cafés. Prenzlauer Berg was the next hot spot following Mitte and is now also quite well established. On the streets, many of Berlin's young crowd chat endlessly on sidewalk cafés and inside mellow clubs. Don't expect outrageous punkiness - it is a lively and intellectual scene that is a delight to explore. Most of the scene is focused around **Kollwitz Platz** and the fire-tower between Diedenhöfer Str. and Kolmarer Str. However, it is also worth venturing over to the wonderful cafés and bars on Winsstrasse and Kastanienallee, and around Helmholtz-platz.

### Kreuzberg

This was the center of anarchy and alternative culture in West Berlin. Kreuzberg is also well-known as being the center of a large Turkish population in Berlin - one of the largest Turkish communities in the world! The mix of immigrants and alternative lifestyles makes for a fascinating, fun, and a vivacious neighborhood. Kreuzberg still holds its own as one of Berlin's most exciting and active areas and is still very much a center of outrageous nightlife, eccentric bars and cafés, and a very youthful, active, and vocal population.

Along the area's most crowded and popular street, **Oranienstrasse**, you will find tons of great nightclubs many great used bookstores, original and unique shops, and endless bars, cafés and restaurants. A particularly prime place to sip a coffee or beer is at one of

### PEGASUS HOSTEL

Str. der Pariser Kommune 35
Dorms €10-14, Private €39-58+;
S: Ostbahnhof (030-29-77-360)
www.pegasushostel.de
*Real Berlin atmosphere and good prices. Pegasus Hostel is situated in central Berlin, just a 5 minute walk from the S-Bahn and long distance train station Ostbahnhof. The famous Berlin Wall is only 5 minute walk from Pegasus Hostel!*

### ST CHRISTOPHER'S INN BERLIN

39-41 Rosa-Luxemburg-Strasse, *Mitte*
Dorms €15+; U/S: Rosa-Luxemburg-Platz. (030-81- 45-39-60)
www.st-christophers.co.uk/berlin
*Ideally located in the exciting and historic Berlin-Mitte. Step up into our hostel where you'll be greeted by our friendly, knowledgeable and multilingual staff, extensive bar and a tasteful restaurant.*

### AMSTEL HOUSE HOSTEL

Waldenserstr. 31.
Dorms €10-12, Private €19-25;
U: Turnstr. (030-39-54-072)
www.amstelhouse.de
*You'll find a warm welcome in our spacious lounge 24 hrs/ day. Our staff will help with all your needs: tourist info, city tours, nightlife tips, laundry service, bike rental or just a beer while you plan your next activity.*

### THE CIRCUS HOSTEL

Weinbergsweg 1a, *Mitte*.
Dorms €19+, Priv. €53+. U: Rosenthaler Platz. (44-208-600-7518)
www.famoushostels.com/berlin-hostel
*The Circus Hostel dominates the "Rosenthaler Platz" in Berlin's pounding heart - "Mitte". The Hostel offers a wide range of accomodation, from a bed in a dorm to the apartments with a breathtaking view over the city.*

**MORE FEATURED HOSTELS ON THE NEXT PAGE**

the cafés around **Heinrichplatz**. Don't just limit yourself to Oranienstrasse. Further south along Wiener Str. and at Spreewaldplatz there is also a great deal to explore.

## Friedrichshain

Berliners say this is the new cutting-edge neighborhood. Further east and far removed from the snazziness of Mitte, Friedrichshain is an old working-class district which is now being filled with students and youth. This area does not have the intensity of Mitte, Prenzlauer Berg or Kreuzberg, but the laid-back and comfortable atmosphere of the various hangouts is really fun and unique. Some of the best streets to explore are **Simon-Dach Str.**, **Wühlisch-strasse**, **Rigaer Str.** and **Schreiner Str.**

## ▶ Museums/Attractions

### Ⓕ Topographie des Terrors

Located behind a large portion of the wall, this is an exhibit of Nazi history at the former site of the Gestapo and SS. Although the information is provided in German only, it is worth a visit and is on the way to Checkpoint Charlie. Admission is free.

### Ⓕ Reichstag

Just past the Brandenburg Gate is the Reichstag, home to the German parliament. The dome on top offers excellent views of Berlin and is also an example of great modern architecture. Open daily until 11pm and is free. Located at Platz der Republik in Tiergarten. S: Unter den Linden.

### Ⓕ Sachsenhausen

This former concentration camp has been turned into a memorial/museum. It served as a "model" concentration camp during the holocaust where over 100,000 people were murdered. After World War II, it was used for political prisoners by the Russians. To get there take the S1 from Friedrichstrasse to Oranienburg (takes about 45 minutes). From there you can walk 15 minutes (2km) to the entrance or take the 804/821 bus. Free admission.

## New Synagogue

Originally opened in 1866, but during the Kristallnacht Pogram in the 1930s the SA tried to burn it down. Due to the building's landmark status, it was spared by the city police but was later destroyed during WWII. From the remains, reconstruction on the synagogue began in 1988 and it was reopened in 1995 as a memorial and museum. Closed Saturdays. Oranienburgerstr 29.

## ▶ Food & Nightlife

The Mitte district is known for its nightlife, but also check out Oderberger Strasse in Prenzlauer Berg for cheap eats and drinks. In general, eating and drinking in "Kniepen", local pubs that serve beer and food, is usually easy on the wallet.

## ▶ Featured Hostels

See **page 111** for a key to hostel icons.

### RIXPACK HOSTEL NEUKÖLLN

Karl-Marx-Str. 75 , *Neukölln* Dorms €12+, Priv. €24+. S: Rathaus Neukölln. (30-5471-5140) www.rixpack.de
*The RIXPACK is the first backpacker hostel in Neukölln, situated in a calm backyard. Subway and night bus just a step away, we offer a safe and good value place to stay. Our vintage building provides dorms and twin rooms.*

### THREE LITTLE PIGS HOSTEL BERLIN

Stresemannstrasse 66, *Potsdamer Platz*Dorms €10+, Priv. €30+. S: Anhalter Bahnhof. (30-26395880) www.three-little-pigs.de
*Visit us in a former convent, right at the "Potsdamer Platz", just minutes away from the pulsing districts of Mitte and Kreuzberg.*

### ALCATRAZ BACKPACKER HOSTEL

Schönhauser Allee 133a, *Prenzlauer Berg*. Dorms €16-18, Priv. €23-40/pp+; M: Schönhauser Allee(030-4849-6815) www.alcatraz-backpacker.de/
*Alcatraz Backpacker Hostel offers a friendly and cozy atmosphere for its international guests. The house was colourfully decorated by local graffiti artists and is a popular photo opportunity both for passers-by and our guests alike.*

### ONE80° HOSTEL BERLIN ALEXANDERPLATZ

Otto-Braun-Strasse 65, *Alexanderplatz* Dorms €14+, Priv. €14+. S/U-Bahn: Alexanderplatz. (49-302-804-4620) www.one80hostels.com
*NEW & just steps away from 'Alex Free WiFi to stay in touch. Comfy rooms, most with bathroom. Bar, Club, Restaurant, 24h reception and Photobooth for funky pics*

## ▶Switzerland

### ▶Zurich

Known as a major financial center, Zurich has more to offer than just bank accounts, businessmen and a stock exchange. Sitting on the Limmat River with a backdrop of the magnificent Swiss Alps, it is a picturesque city that, thanks to its significant wealth and central geographical location, is alive with culture and lots to do.

Enjoy a more traditional Swiss atmosphere in Neiderdorf, the ancient medieval section of the city, complete with narrow cobblestones streets and charming eateries. But also indulge in the very cosmopolitan vibe exhibited throughout the entire city from varied personalities, art exhibits, bars and a hyped club scene. **To See/Do**: Paradeplatz (square), Kunsthaus (gallery), Neiderdorf, rent a paddle boat on the lake.

### ▶Interlaken Region

The Swiss version of Austria's Innsbruck, Interlaken is, in a word, idyllic. Set in the Bernese Oberland, it is surrounded by snow capped mountains, blue lakes, cow bells, swiss chalets and of course lots of tourists, which should by no means be a deterrent. Visitors can easily avoid each other in this vast spectacular landscape for the couple of days you may spend here. Interlaken is the largest and central town of the region.

### ▶Lauterbrunnen

Fields of wildflowers, snow-capped mountains and fresh mountain air await you in Lauterbrunnen, a picturesque Swiss village with awe-inspiring scenery and a friendly populace.

Waterfalls abound in this region, and you can wander amongst the sheer mountain slopes to hunt them down for a morning excursion or afternoon picnic. Set in one of the Alps' deepest valleys, Lauterbrunnen offers spectacular scenery, ice-cold rivers and forests out of a fairy tale.

### ▶Lucerne

Swans like to call Lucerne home, and it's easy to understand why. Set beside a gorgeous (and freezing cold) glacial lake, this Swiss village has mountain views, a restored medieval covered bridge and pretty flower-covered windowsills everywhere.

Hike into the surrounding mountains, rent a paddleboat on the lake or wander the winding

## ▶Quick Facts

**Calling Information**

*Country Code*: Austria 43, Switzerland 41

*Calling in Austria/Switzerland*: add a "0" before the area code

*Calling overseas*: 00+country code+area code+number

**Currency & Exchange Rates**

*Currency*: Euro (€) in Austria, Swiss Franc in Switzerland

*Exchange Rates*: €1 costs: US$1.30/ £.81/AUD$1.24/ CAN$1.28

*Exchange Rates*: 1SF costs: US$1.07/ £.67/AUD$1.02/CAN$1.06/€.83

## ▶Featured Hostels

See **page 111** for a key to hostel icons.

### BACKPACKERS VILLA SONNENHOF

Alpenstrasse 16, *Interlaken, Switzerland*. Dorms €32.50+, Private €41+/pp. (033-826-7171) www.villa.ch
*Backpackers Villa Sonnenhof is the perfect base for those looking for the comfort and convenience of a centrally located Interlaken hostel that provides just that little extra.*

### LAUSANNE BACKPACKERS

Chemin des Epinettes 4, *Lausanne, Switzerland*. Dorms CHF36.40+, Priv. CHF106+. (021-601-8000) www.lausanne-guesthouse.ch
*The hotel with charm. A restored old townhouse that complies with the strictest ecological standards. Friendly atmosphere. Free bus/metro and train ticket in Lausanne area included.*

streets. Lucerne is a great place to try traditional Swiss cuisine like raclette or fondue – and save your extra breadcrumbs for the swans.

## ⸙Austria

### ⸙Salzburg

The birthplace of Mozart and the site of Julie Andrews' Sound of Music, Salzburg remains a city of music, culture and art. At every turn you can either tire of, or indulge in the genius of Mozart (tours, museums etc.) and play out the splendor of the Sound of Music (tours, memorabilia etc.)

Aside from being inundated with these two Salzburg claims to fame, the city is truly beautiful and picturesque. Rimmed with views of the beautiful Alps, its Baroque character is perfectly preserved in its magnificent architecture, including beautiful palaces, abbeys and museums. **To See/Do**: Mozart Square and birthplace, Schloss Mirabell, Residenz, Festung Hohensalzburg.

### ⸙Vienna

Vienna surpasses her Austrian counterparts when it comes to culture, art and history. Once the mecca of European culture in the 18th and 19th centuries, hosting all the great musical geniuses from Beethoven to Mozart, you can't help but still feel the richness and grandeur of a once glorious empire.

Amidst beautiful historic Baroque architecture there also exists a modern-day culture that invites you to take part in a lively and thriving youth scene. Whether you spend an afternoon in a traditional kaffehaus or take part in the cool club and bar scene, you will have the best of both old and new. **To See/Do**: Osterreichische Galerie Belvedere (palace), Hundertwasserhaus, Museum of Fine Arts.

### ⸙Innsbruck

With images of lederhosen, yodelers, endless snow-capped mountains and pretty little villages, the Tirol region is post-card-perfect. In the winter this is the premier destination for avid skiers, particularly Innsbruck, which has many excellent resorts.

In the summer, feast on glorious greenery, mountain lakes and superb hiking trails. The main central town of Innsbruck is filled with much history, culture, folklore and natural beauty, making it an excellent base to explore the entire region.

## ⸙Add'l Hostels

### ⸙Switzerland

**Bern Backpackers**
Rathausgasse 75, *Bern*
(031-211-3771)

**Swiss Adventures**
Hotel Baeren, Hauptstr., *Boltigen*
(033-773-7373)

**City Hostel Geneva**
Rue Ferrier 2, *Geneva*,
(022-901-1500)

**Mountain Hostel Gimmelwald**
Terrassenweg, *Gimmelwald*
(033-853-3900)

**Swiss Alps Retreat**
*Gryon*. (024-498-3321)

**Balmer's Herberge**
Haupstrasse 23, *Interlaken*
(033-822-1961)

**Lucerne Youth Hostel**
Sedelstrasse 12, *Lucerne*
(41-420-8800)

**Riviera Lodge**
Place du Marché 5, Vevey
(021-923-8040)

**Matterhorn Hostel**
*Zermatt*. (027-968-1919)

**Zermatt Youth Hostel**
"Winkelmatten", Staldenweg 5,
*Zermatt*. (27-967-2320)

**City Backpacker/Hotel Biber**
Niederdorfstrasse 5, *Zurich*
(43-251-9015)

**Zurich Youth Hostel**
Mutschellenstrasse 114, *Zurich*
(43-399-7800)

### ⸙Austria

**Treehouse Backpacker Hotel**
Schindlbachstr. 525, *Grunau*
(076-16-84-99)

**Youth Hostel Innsbruck**
Reichenauerstr. 147, *Innsbruck*
(0512-346-179 )

**Yoho Int'l Hotel & Hostel**
Paracelsusstr 9, *Salzburg*
(0662-879-649)

**Hostel Ruthensteiner**
Robert Hamerlinggasse 24,
*Vienna* (01-893-4202)

**Wombats Hostel**
Grangasse 6, *Vienna*.
(01-897-2336)

# ▶Eastern Eur...
# & Scandinavia

FINLAND

NORWAY

Oslo★

Helsinki

St. Petersburg

SWEDEN

Stockholm★

Tallinn★

Gothenburg

ESTONIA
Tartu

Moscow★

DENMARK

Riga

RUSSIA

Arhus
Copenhagen

Malmo

Liepaja

★ LATVIA

Baltic Sea

LITHUANIA

Berlin ★

Gdansk

Vilnius★

Minsk

BELARUS

GERMANY

POLAND

Warsaw

Lodz•

Krakow

Kiev
★

UKRAINE

Prague ★

CZECH REP.

SLOVAKIA

Vienna ★★Bratislava

AUSTRIA

★ Budapest

HUNGARY

SLOVENIA★Ljubljana

ROMANIA

★Zagreb

Brasov

ITALY

CROATIA

Belgrade

Bucharest

BOSNIA

HERG

SERBIA

Black Sea

Sarajevo

Sofia

Varna

(MONT.)

BULGARIA

Rome★

Tirana

Skopje

MAC.

Istanbul★

ALBANIA

Thessalonika

Ankara

Corfu

GREECE

TURKEY

Izmir

Konya•

Athens

Nauplione

Mediterranean Sea

Kalamata•

Rodhos•

Rodhes

Cyprus

| 0 | 210 | 420 Miles |
| 0 | 210 | 420 KM |

Crete •

• Iraklion

...s one of the most
...ceful nature of the
...hed by wars. And,
...e city's seemingly
...ly labored over for
...ctacular and beauti-
...the city of fairy tales
- a city ... ...uck that nearly every
street could be the ... ...hey have ever seen.

Beware though - countless visitors have flocked from around the world to Prague's beautiful, narrow streets. More than any other city in Europe, the strains of a booming tourist industry are evident, especially during the summer. Authentic Czech restaurants and cafés are difficult to find. It is hard to hear Czech spoken and the energy of the city is often more akin to a tourist resort than that of the cultural, political, and financial center of a growing European nation.

But don't let the other tourists scare you away. Prague is still ridiculously cheap! If you step just a block or two away from the popular tourist spots, you will find that the old-world sparkle of Prague still shines brightly. The amazing buildings, squares, and streets alone are enough to alter one's view of the world. Once you have seen Prague, your perception of beauty will be forever changed.

## Getting There

Prague is centrally located: only 5 hours south of Berlin, 4.5 hours north of Vienna, 8 hours northeast of Budapest and 11.5 hours east of Zurich. It is a popular stop on the Vienna/Budapest/Prague travel route.

### From the Airport

Prague is well-serviced by international flights at the sleek and comfortable **Ruzyne Airport**. Here, flights arrive from and depart for all parts of Europe on nearly all major European airlines.

The **Cedaz** shuttle bus operates from the airport to V Celnici Street in the city center from 7:30am-7pm for 130k and takes 20-30 minutes. The Airport Express Bus (AE) goes to Prague's main bus station for 60k. **Public bus #119** costs 32k and goes to Dejvická station where you can catch the metro green line into Prague city center.www.prg.aero/en/

### Coach & Rail

Prague is extremely well-serviced by international train lines. There are daily services from Krakow, Warsaw, Bratislava, Budapest, Berlin, Nuremburg, Munich, and Vienna.

## Visitor Info
www.czech.cz/en/
See page 105 for a Prague city map

## Quick Facts
### Calling Information
*Country Code*: 420

*Calling in Czech Republic*: add a "0" before the area code

*Calling overseas*: 00+country code+area code+number

### Currency & Exchange Rates
*Currency*: Korunas (k)

*Currency Breakdown*: 100 haleru (h) equals 1k

*Exchange Rates*: 10k costs: US$.51 /£.32/AUD$.49/CAN$.51/€.40

### Must See/Must Do
Absinthe, Prague Castle, Mala Strana

### Say What!
Thank you=Dekuji ; Where is=Kde je...?; How much is it=Kolik to stoji?

## Notes

_____

_____

_____

_____

_____

_____

_____

_____

_____

_____

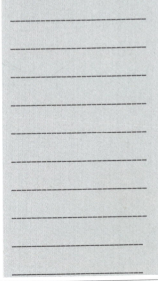

The two main stations are **Praha hlavní nádrazí** and **Hole-sovice**. Hlavní nádrazí handles most main international routes, although many also leave from Holesovice. Make sure you know which station your train leaves from. Both stations are easily accessible by the Metro C to Hlavní nádrazí station and to Nádrazí Holesovice station, respectively. The largest of Prague's bus stations is **Florenc**, located at Krizíkova 4 (Metro B, C: Florenc).

## ▶Getting Around

As everything is within walking distance, you can probably spend most of your visit to Prague without using public transport. Alternatively, you can use Prague's extensive and efficient metro system that has 3 lines. There are also various trams and buses that fill the metro's gaps. All three systems share the same tickets. The metro runs daily from 5am-midnight. At night, trams #51-58 and various night buses operate (marked in blue at bus stops).

The ticketing system is somewhat confusing and prices change based on rush hour times as well as distance and time traveling. The standard single fare is 24k for a 30 minute trip or 32k for 90 minute trip. We recommend purchasing one of the **travel passes** which cost 110k for a 24-hour pass and 310k for a 3-day pass. Tickets may be purchased at each station or at newsstands. You must validate (stamp) your ticket as you board the tram and bus or as you enter the metro paid areas. Once validated, you can transfer for free within that hour (1.5 hrs after 8pm) to different buses, trams, metros, etc. www.dpp.cz/en/fares-in-prague/

## ▶Things to See & Do

### ▶Tourist Information

The main tourist office is located in the Old Town Hall at Staroměstské náměstí. Other branches are at Prahahlavní nádrazí train station, Rytirska 31, and in the tower on the Malá Strana side of the Charles Bridge.

### ▶Neighborhoods
#### Stare Mesto

This is the most historic part of the city where you can find the **Old Town Hall**, **Old Town Square** and many beautiful, narrow, winding medieval streets.

#### Hradcany

Also known as **Castle Hill**, this is where much of Czech history unfolded and today is one of the most splendid (and visited) neighborhoods. Two of the most beautiful and distinct streets are **Novy Svet** and **Zlatá ulicka**.

#### Malá Strana

Located across the **Charles Bridge** from Stare Mesto, it is here that the romantic and stunning beauty of Prague is most intensely felt. The inti-

## ▶Featured Hostels

See **page 111** for a key to hostel icons

### ARPACAY BACKPACKERS
Nerudova 40
Dorms €7.50+; Private €16pp;
Tram: Malostranske namesti.
(0251-552-297)
www.arpacayhostel.com
*Located in the picturesque Nerudova street right below Prague Castle. Sleep in a unique historical building from the 16th century and enjoy an amazing view over the Lesser Town. Beds from 10 EUR.*

### ST CHRISTOPHER'S INN PRAGUE
Mosaic House, Odboru 4
Dorms €15+; T: metro line B to Karlovo namesti. (0221-595-351)
www.st-christophers.co.uk/prague-hostels
*Quite simply the best hostel in Prague is St Christopher's @ Mosaic House, mere minutes from all the sights along the river. We're within walking distance of all the major attractions and we couldn't be easier to find.*

### CZECH INN
Francouzska 76
Dorms €11+; Private €38pp;
Metro: Tram #4 or 22 to Krymska.
(44-208-600-7518)
www.famoushostels.com/prague-hostel
*Czech Inn presents hotel-quality facilities and services at hostel prices. Guests can experience the richness of Prague's architectural history in this beautifully restored 19th century building while being able to enjoy the comfort of a modern-design hostel.*

mate scale, combined with many trees and beautiful quaint buildings, creates an atmosphere that begs for people to fall in love with each other and the city itself. The most picturesque streets are: Na Kampe, Misenska, Velko-prevorské námestí, Nerudova and Thunovska. Beware, however, the restaurants here are pricey.

### Nove Mesto
The neighborhood of Nove Mesto is far less touristed but much more vibrant. It is on these streets that contemporary Czech life can be discovered. Particularly good streets include **V jirchárich** and **Kremencova**.

### Petrin Hill
One of the most beautiful things to do in Prague is to look out over all of the fantastic domes, spires, and bright red roofs. One of the best places, and the cheapest, is from the paths on Petrin Hill, where a mix of gardens and paths shoot up behind the Mala Strana neighborhood next to the castle. It is a very popular place among locals for strolls and a great place for visitors to relax and absorb the breathtaking view.

### Vysehrad
One of the most historic areas in the city. Legend says that from these rocky crags above the Vlatva, Countess Libuse first envisioned the great city of Prague and set out to find a king for Bohemia. The area still retains some of this mythical character and is very dear to Czech hearts. At the graveyard here some of the most famous Czechs now rest, including Dvorak.

Besides the graveyard, there is a fantastic park and a haunting, yet beautiful, black Romanesque church. Admission to the whole area is free. Vysehrad is also where some of the best examples of Czech cubist architecture can be found. Check out the buildings at Neklanova 30, Libusina 3, and a villa on Rasinovo nabrezi. To get to Vysehrad, take the Metro C line to the Vysehrad stop and then walk west towards the river.

### Kampa
Kampa is one of the islands in the Vltava River, although it doesn't feel much like an island — it is separated from Mala Strana by only the thin Certovka canal. On the island is a beautiful leafy park where people from all over the city and the world gather to relax. Drumming circles, Frisbee games and picnics are not uncommon. This is a great place to escape from the hordes of tourists on nearby Charles Bridge and soak up the laid-back youthful energy of Prague.

### ▶Food & Nightlife

The Zizkov district is lined with bars and pubs of all sorts. In addition, check out *Think*, an English-language publication of the city's hip happenings.

**▶Notes**

# ▶Budapest

**BUDAPEST**, the capital of Hungary, is an interesting, cosmopolitan city that should not be underestimated. Budapest's beautiful historic section is Castle Hill on the Buda side of the Danube. Across the river is Pest, the sprawling and hectic center of the modern city that saw much of its development at the turn of century.

Budapest is possibly more active, enticing, and bewildering than any other European city. Here, business people from as far as Moscow and London brush shoulders on the subway while youth from all over the world enjoy the city's many great cafés, bars and clubs. It's a gritty city still left to its locals and savored for its pounding, pensive energy.

## ▶Getting There

Budapest, a popular stop on the Vienna/Budapest/Prague travel route by rail, is located 10.5 hours south of Krakow, 3 hours southeast of Vienna and 7-9 hours southeast of Prague.

### ▶From the Airport

**Ferihegy Airport**, located 20km south east of Budapest, is serviced by public bus #200E or #93 to Kobánya-Kispest metro station where you can change to the M3 metro for other stops within Budapest (from 320Ft). Note the last metro leaves at 11:00pm, after which you must take the #909 or 999 night bus. www.bud.hu/english

### ▶Bus & Rail

MAV is the Hungarian national rail carrier. Budapest is one of the most important European rail junctions. From here you can catch a train to Venice, Istanbul, Warsaw and Paris. The word for train station in Hungarian is *pályaudvar*, abbreviated "pu." The three main stations in the city are **Keleti pu.**, **Nyugati pu.**, and **Deli pu**. Most international trains arrive and depart from Keleti pu. Both Keleti pu. and Deli pu. are stops on the M2 metro line, while Nyugati pu. lies on the M3 line. For good discounts on tickets, see IBUSZ tours, whose central branch is at Ferenciek tér 10 (M3 Ferenciek tér).

Most buses to and from Western Europe use **Volánbusz** Népliget coach station, located at Ülloi út 131 (Red metro line to the Stadionok stop). Most buses to Eastern European destinations leave from Népstadion station, located at Hungária körút 48/52.

## ▶Getting Around

Budapest has an extremely comprehensive public transportation network. There are three crisscrossing metro lines, complemented by many trams and

## ▶Visitor Info

www.budapestinfo.hu/en/

See page 106 for a Budapest city map

## ▶Quick Facts

**Calling Information**
*Country Code*: 36

*Calling in Hungary*: add a "06" before the area code

*Calling overseas*: 00+country code+area code+number

**Currency & Exchange Rates**
*Currency*: Forint (ft)

*Currency Breakdown*: 100 filler (f) equals 1 ft

*Exchange Rates*: 100ft costs: US$.46 / £.28/ AUD$.44/ CAN$.45/€.35

**Must See/Must Do**
Thermal Baths, Castle Hill, Coffee Houses

**Say What!**
Where is=Hol van...?; How much is it=Mennyibe kerül?; Do you speak English=Beszél angolul?

## ▶Notes

_____

_____

_____

_____

_____

_____

_____

_____

buses. You must have a validated ticket (320Ft single fare) for every trip, including transfers from one subway, bus, or tram line to another and transfers between each separate mode of transit. **Day passes** cost 1550Ft and a 3-day tourist ticket is 3850Ft. The subways shut down around midnight but the city is well serviced by an efficient night bus system (begins with # 9). Day passes work at night, otherwise buy a single ticket on the bus. www.bkv.hu/en/

## ▶Things to See & Do

### ▶Tourist Information
For comprehensive advice, visit info points at the airport and Liszt Ferenc tér at Andrássy útca 47.

### ▶Areas & Attractions
### Castle Hill
The only part of Budapest that one might really call "pretty." The reconstructed area is made up of pastel colored baroque houses, the beautiful **Matyás Church** and the city's historic castle. This is, however, where very few of the city's 2 million residents live or go out; this is almost exclusively a tourist center.

### Andrassy Útca
For a tour of Budapest history walk down Andrassy Útca. Along this street you will pass the city **Opera House**, many historic cafés from the turn of the century, and at the end, you will reach Hero's Square and City Park. This is the street the Soviet tanks rolled down in 1956.

### Public Thermal Baths
Budapest is the only European capital city that resides over constantly flowing thermal waters. A must do for any visitor is to take a break from the bustle of the city and relax in one of the many public thermal baths. Gellért baths are the most famous, but Széchenyi baths in City Park are also wonderful, less touristed and always co-ed and straight. Széchenyi Baths cost 2900-3950ft, Gellért costs 3200-4600ft, and Rudas costs 1900-3600ft.

### Margaret Island
For respite from the pollution and mayhem of Budapest's streets, head to either Margaret Island (Margitsziget) or City Park (Városliget). Margaret Island, located smack in the middle of the Danube, is a beautiful mix of open fields and lush gardens. It is a great way to truly see the grandeur and beauty of the Danube. It is accessed via the Margaret Bridge (Margit Hid) by buses 26 or 26A.

## ▶Food & Nightlife

As one of the cheapest cities in Europe, take advantage of Budapest's culture and finer luxuries. Treat yourself to classical music or opera as well as fine dining. Go to Liszt Ferenc Ter for bar/café hopping.

## ▶Featured Hostels
See **page 111** for a key to hostel icons.

### ANADIN FEMALE HOSTEL
54. Pozsonyi út ground floor 4 (doorbell 4). Dorms €11.50+ (3670-243-5391)
www.budapestyouthhostel.com
*At last! A hostel for you ladies! Budapest's 1 and only 1 female hostel Anadin hostel is a clean, safe, cozy and comfortable place for female travelers. Free use of hairdryer, internet and wi-fi, and breakfast is also included!*

### MAVERICK HOSTEL
Ferenciek tere 2
Dorms €11+; Private €22+/pp
(44-208-600-7518)
www.famoushostels.com/budapest-hostel
*The hostel is located incredibly centrally, just moments away from the Danube, giving you maximum time to spend discovering this magnificent city, often cited as one of the most beautiful of Europe.*

## ▶Additional Hostels
**7x27 Hostel**
14. Kiraly u, 36
(20-9999-724)

**Aquarium Youth Hostel 1076**
Alsoerdosor utca 12 2nd fl
(1-322-0502)

**Bakfark Backpackers Hostel**
Bakfark Balint u 1; M 2: Moszkva tér
(1-340-8585)

**Best Hostel**
Podmaniczky u 27; M 3: Nyugati Pu
(1-332-4934)

**Hostel Marco Polo**
Nyár Utca 6; M: Blaha Lujza tér
(1-413-2555)

**Traveller's Hostel Banki**
Podmaniczky u 8; M 3: Nyugati Pu (1-329-8644)

**Yellow Submarine Youth Hostel**
Terez Körut 56
(1-269-4354)

# ▶▶Turkey

Turkey is a land for anyone seeking an uncommon holiday. It is a land of mystery and deep historical significance, rich in culture and robust in modern infrastructure. When you visit Turkey, you stand where civilization began. Turkey is more often than not considered three countries in one. It has unmatched diversity of geography, architecture and landscape. The west coast of Turkey offers a wide range of sites and activities for the traveler, from trekking, hiking, sailing, diving, paragliding, skiing and hot air ballooning to partaking in traditional Turkish folklore evenings and shopping in many of the local street markets.

The East is untouched by tourism and offers more genuine experiences while still playing host to some of history's most interesting and religious sites, including Ishak Pasa Palace in Dogubeyazit overlooking Mt. Ararat; the mystical van cats with one green and one blue eye; the former Armenian capital of Ani; Akdamar Island and the Holy Cross Church on Turkey's largest lake; the mud huts of Urfa; the stone heads of the gods at Mt Nemrut; and the first church known to man in Antakya.

The Black Sea Coast, often referred to as the Emerald Coast, offers a lush, green and fertile environment. Along Turkey's northern coast you can visit such places as Trabzon, which plays host to the Sumela Monastery, built on a sheer cliff face; the boat-making village of Sinop; the traditional Ottoman Houses in Safranbolu; or the beach in Sile. Turkey is literally the bridge where East meets West, both physically and culturally.

## ▶▶Getting There

### ▶▶Rail

Trains are not a recommended method of travel in Turkey. The two major lines run from Istanbul to Ankara and Istanbul to Denizli. Both are twice as slow as bus transport and a little more expensive.

### ▶▶By Car

Renting a car will give you more flexibility and freedom but be aware that Turkey has the worst statistics for casualties on roads than any other nation and fuel is quite expensive, currenty around €2 per litre.

## ▶▶Getting Around

### ▶▶Backpacker Tours

**Fez Travel**

Fez Travel offers tours around Turkey and Greece including the 10 day Magic Carpet tour ($895-1159)

## ▶▶Web Links

**Visitor Information**
www.tourismturkey.org

## ▶▶Quick Facts

**Calling Information**
*Country Code*: 90

*Calling in Turkey*: add a "0" before the area code

*Calling overseas*: 00+country code+area code+number

**Currency & Exchange Rates**
*Currency*: New Turkish Lira (equals 1 million old lira) or USD (widely used in Turkey)

*Currency Breakdown*: 1 New Turkish Lira equals 100 kurus.

*Exchange Rates*: 1 lira costs US$.56/€.43/£.35/AUD$.53/CAN$.55

**Say What!**
How much?=kac para?
How are you?=Nasil-siniz?
Do you speak English?=Ingilizce biliyor musunuz?

## ▶▶Highlights

Istanbul, Gallipoli, Ephesus ruins, Cappadocia, Turkish markets

## ▶▶Notes

_____

_____

_____

_____

_____

or the 12 day Orient Express ($1,439). Both include hotel, meals and transport but exclude kitty payment. They also offer budget Fez Bus Tours around Western Turkey including their 14-day Turkish Delight Tour ($869US). The 6-day Aegean Trail Tour costs $499US. www.feztravel.com

## Travel Talk Tours

Offers a 9-day "Essential Turkey" adventure tours for independent travelers. Costs from £249 and includes coach transport, accommodation and breakfast. See Istanbul, Gallipoli, Troy, Pergamum, Ephesus, Cappadocia, Ankara and more. (90-212-522-5468). www.traveltalktours.com

## ▶Bus

Frequent, modern and cheap buses run between cities, towns and villages of all sizes. There can be over 1,000 bus networks operating throughout Turkey at any one time. For longer journeys, it is recommended to use one of the more reputable companies such as Ulusoy, Varan or Kamil Koc. These companies are generally more expensive but offer greater comfort.

Local bus tickets can be purchased from any travel agency in any city or town, or direct from the bus station. When booking with an agency in Istanbul, make sure you are offered a free transfer to the bus station.

## ▶Dolmus

A dolmus, a mini van used for public transport, will take you from one small town to another or from suburb to suburb within a town. There are no set dolmus stops so you are expected to wave them down as they pass. Make sure you look on the front or side of the vehicle for names of places the dolmus will visit. You are free to jump off the dolmus at any time by signaling the driver to stop (dur).

## ▶Istanbul

**Sultanahmet**, the old city of Istanbul, plays host to the majority of tourist sites. All are within a short walking distance of each other. Start with the Topkapi Palace, Blue Mosque, Saint Sophia Museum, Hippodrome, Underground Cistern, Grand Bazaar and Egyptian Spice Markets.

If these aren't enough, get out of touristville and visit the Dolmabahce Palace, Camlica Hill (highest point in Istanbul on the Asian side), cruise up the Bosphorus (stretch of water separating Europe from Asia) or check out the Prince's Islands in the Marmara Sea. If it's bars you're after, Akbiyik Caddesi is lined with cafés and bars, but if you wish to go where the locals go, try Taksim or Ortakoy.

## ▶HOSTELS

### ▶Istanbul

**Amphora Hostel**
Binbirdirek Mah Su Terazisi sok 8, *Sultanahmet* (0212-638-1554)

**Orient Youth Hostel**
Akbiyik Caddes 13, *Sultanahmet* (0212-518-0879)

**Anadolu Hostel**
Salkim Sogut Sok, *Sultananahmet* (0212-512-1035)

**Istanbul Hostel**
35 Kutlu Gun Sokak, *Sultananahmet* (0212-516-9380)

**Sinbad Youth Hostel**
Demirci Resit Sok 3, *Sultanahmet* (0212-638-2721)

**Sultan Hostel**
Akbiyik Cad. No. 21 Terbiyik Sok 3, *Sultanahmet* (0212-516-9260)

**Yucelt Inter Youth Hostel**
Caferiye Sok. No 6/1, *Sultanahmet* (0212-513-6150)

**Cordial House Hotel/Pension**
Peykhane Sokak 29, *Cemberlitas* (0212-517-2727)

### ▶Gallipoli

**Anafartalar Hotel**
Canakkale Ferry Port, *Canakkale* (0286-217-4454)

**ANZAC House Youth Hostel**
Cumhuriyet Meydani No. 61, *Canakkale* (0286-213-5969)

**Boss II Hotel**
Ataturk Caddesi, *Eceabat* (0286-814-2311)

### ▶Selcuk/Izmir

**ANZ Guesthouse**
1064 Sk #12, *Selcuk* (0232-892-6050)

**Ephesus Inn**
14 Mayis mah Kobuleti cad No:40, *Selcuk* (0232-892-3736)

### ▶Kusadasi

**Hotel Sammy's Place**
Kibris Cad No 14, *Kusadasi* (0256-612-2588)

### ▶Koycegiz

**Tango Pension**
Ali Ihsan Kalmaz Cad, Ulu Cami Mah, *Koycegiz* (0252-262-2501)

## ⇒Gallipoli

Highly recommended is the tour of Gallipoli with Professor Kenan Celik of Trooper Tours.

## ⇒Selcuk/Izmir

The ruins of Ephesus is a must see in this area! Selcuk is the closest village to the ruins, but most hostels/hotels offer free lifts from Kusadasi as well. Inside, you'll see, among the ruins, the Grand Theatre and Celcus Library, the first advertisement known to man.

One of the Seven Wonders of the Ancient World lies in the Temple of Artemis opposite the bottom gate of Ephesus. Nearby is the cave of the seven sleepers. The Greek village of Sirince, 4km from Selcuk, plays host to some Turkey's funkiest wines. Also check out the trekking opportunities in the Finger Mountains.

## ⇒Kusadasi

Kusadasi, a more commercialized town, is a great place to party. Bar Street is just a short walk from all major accommodation places, but be warned it can be a little expensive! For good swimming, Kusadasi has some excellent beaches. Check out Ladies and Green Beaches.

Kusadasi is also a port town for the Greek Islands. If you're thinking about island hopping, then this is the place you would no doubt want to depart from.

## ⇒Pamukkale

The Cotton Castles are said to have existed for over thousands of years. This natural phenomenon is the only must see in this tiny village. The ruins of Hierapolis, which lie overlooking the calcium terraces, are also worth a look.

## ⇒Marmaris

Jump on board a gulet (yacht) from Marmaris to Fethiye for 4 days and live like a king or queen. This is by far the best option available here and if you have time, it really shouldn't be missed!

## ⇒Koycegiz

Koycegiz, translated, means small poor village. It is slowly becoming a highlight on the backpacker and independent travelers' scene. There are many options here for the adventurous spirited traveler. Jump on a boat to Turtle Beach, where you can visit the mud baths and the Caunos ruins.

Head to 'The Waterfall', just a mile or two out of Koycegiz, where the natural flowing stream is a

## ⇒Fethiye/Oludeniz
**Ferah Hostel**
2 Karagozler Ordu Cad No 21, *Fethiye* (0252-614-2816)

**Ideal Hostel Pension**
Karagozler Mahallesi Zafer Caddesi, No:6, *Fethiye* (0252-614-1981)

**Oludeniz Camping**
Oludeniz
(0252-617-0048)

## ⇒Olympos
**Kadir's Top Tree Houses**
Olympos, *Antalya*
(0242-892-1250)

**Orange Pension**
Yazir Koyu, Olympos, *Antalya*
(0242-892-1242)

## ⇒Cappadocia
**Flinstones Cave Motel Pension**
Goreme, *Cappadocia*
(0384-271-2525)

**Kelebek Motel-Pension**
Goreme, *Cappadocia*
(0384-271-2531)

**Sururi's Place Pension**
Goreme, *Cappadocia*
(0384-271-2307)

**Tuna Pension**
Goreme, *Cappadocia*
(0384-271-2681)

## ⇒Notes

_____

_____

_____

_____

_____

_____

_____

_____

_____

great place to swim and jump off the rocks. Whitewater raft down the Dalaman River where rapids can reach up to Grade 4. Or feed your sweet tooth with home-made ice cream sold near the center of town.

## ▸▸Fethiye/Oludeniz

If it's adventure you're after, this is the place you've been seeking. From Fethiye (port town) you can jump on a yacht (gulet) from here and either sail to Olympos for four days (highly recommended) or spend three days on board back to Fethiye. There are numerous water sports available. Alternatively, you can catch a boat out to Butterfly Valley (the only home to the Jersey Tiger butterfly) and chill out on the platforms, which are available to sleep on.

Oludeniz is popular spot for paragliding for which it is rated the second best place in the world. If you're keen to jump off a cliff with a parachute strapped to your back from 2000 meters, this is the place. Other area activities include the deserted village of Kayakoyu, close to Oludeniz, and a day trip to Saklikent Gorge for a trek of a lifetime.

## ▸▸Kas

This village offers some great shopping as well as daily boat trips to the sunken city of Kekova. You can also paraglide here or hire a sea kayak for the day and paddle in the Med!

## ▸▸Olympos

The eternal flames of Chimeara are a must see! Most accommodation places offer nightly tours for less than $3US. You may need a torch as you will have to trek up the hill to access the site. Check out the ruins of Olympos, close to the beach. The small fee is worth the fun you will have finding the ancient city hidden in the scrub. Daily boat trips are also available with several opportunities to swim.

## ▸▸Cappadocia

The surreal land of Cappadocia offers tons of activities for every type of traveler. This is the most visited place in Turkey and after you arrive, you'll know why! Open-air museums and Underground cities are a must see, as is Rose Valley and Uchisar Castle. While in Cappadocia, make sure you check out Selimiye, where they filmed the beginning of the original Star Wars film. Also try a traditional Turkish folklore evening featuring belly dancers, folk dancers and food. Adventure seekers should take a ride in a hot air balloon, a favorite among most travelers, as is hiring a moped for the day and exploring the region independently.

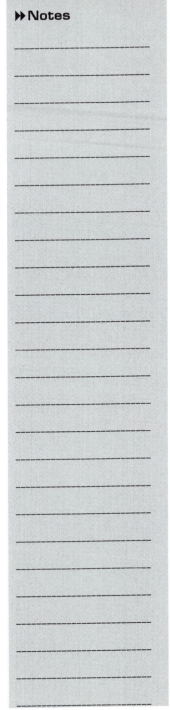

## ▸▸Notes

# ▶Greece

## ▶Corfu

The "Emerald Island" is the most tropical of all the Greek isles. Cliffs of lush greenery and sloping hills plunge into sun drenched beaches and blue azure waters. Without losing its hospitable and entertaining character, this delightful island has more of a pastoral feel than the other, more arid, Greek islands such as Ios and Santorini. Several resorts are ideally tucked into the nooks of seaside hills - from popular and lively accommodations, such as the renowned Pink Palace, to more intimate and peaceful lodgings. You can always find something to suit your tastes/needs. Nightlife is mainly centered in town, so pretty much everyone's there...meaning it can get somewhat raucous! Corfu is a little bit of everything for just about everyone.

## ▶IOS

Sort of like the never-ending Mardi Gras of the Mediterranean, Ios is a place where you party 'til dawn and sleep it off on the beach with a beer in your hand. The small whitewashed town of Chora, perched high on a hill, is the center of it all. Lots of bars, cafés and nightclubs are clustered together amidst beautiful churches and squares. At night the small cobblestone streets are teeming with zealous partygoers from all over the world. During the day, relax on the beach or rent a small moped and tour the island taking in the magnificent views of the surrounding sea, cliffs and occasional palm tree.

## ▶Santorini

Hauntingly beautiful, Santorini is justifiably the most photographed of all the Greek islands. Its serene beauty and intrinsically Mediterranean flavor subtly and calmly seeps into your senses. The result of past volcano eruptions created a dramatic jagged coastline contrasted by the deep blue Aegean sea and sunny sandy beaches. Picture perfect whitewashed villages carved into steep cliffs sit atop some of the most spectacular views. There are 11 different towns to check out, especially Ia (striking coastline and quaint village with museums, bars, cafés and beach) and Thira/Fira (magnificent architecture, bars, discos etc). Note that Santorini is the most southern of all the Greek islands (9 hour ferry ride from Piraeus).

## ▶Olympia

The sprawling ruins here are a UNESCO World Heritage site. They include the Olympic Arena and the Temple of Zeus, which once housed the colossal gold-and-ivory cult statue of Zeus (one of the seven wonders of the ancient world).

## ▶Visitor Info

www.visitgreece.gr

## ▶Quick Facts

**Calling Information**

*Country Code*: 30; *Calling in Greece*: add a "0" before the area code; *Calling overseas*: 00+country code+area code+number

**Currency & Exchange Rates**

*Currency*: Euro (€)

*Exchange Rates*: €1 costs: US$1.30/ £.81/AUD$1.24/ CAN$1.28

## ▶Featurd Hostels

**THE PINK PALACE HOSTEL**
Agios Gordios Beach, *Corfu*
Dorms €18+, Private €30+;
(0266-10 5-3103)
www.thepinkpalace.com
*For the backpacker or jet setter, The Pink Palace is sure to suit every travel budget. Whether you are looking for a fulfilling adventure holiday or a relaxing get-away, you will find it here.*

**CORFU BACKPACKERS**
Agios Gordios Beach, *Corfu*
Dorms €18+, Private €30+;
(694-5230727)
www.corfubackpackers.com
*Corfu Backpackers Inn is located on the west coast of Corfu, beside the long sandy beach of Agios Gordios with its amazing sunsets and variety of water sports. It is the perfect place for a cheap Corfu beach holiday.*

# ▸▸Athens

ATHENS is one of the few cities in the world in which the installation of a modern metro system is regularly halted by important archaeological discoveries; the artifacts are now on display in its stations. Above the Athens skyline, the Acropolis reigns supreme: brightly lit by night, chock-full of awestruck tourists by day, it is but one of the many ancient and modern treasures that this versatile city – much improved since hosting the 2004 Olympics – provides.

## ▸▸Getting There

### ▸▸From the Airport

**Athens International Airport** is a 20-minute metro ride from the city center. Express buses connect the airport to Piraeus (X96), the metro station at Dafni (X97) and the Kifissos coach station (X93). Tickets are €5. You can also take Metro Line 3 or the suburban railway to the city center for €8. The new 3-day tourist ticket (€15) includes the metro and bus from the airport to Athens.

### ▸▸Boat, Coach & Rail

Trains to and from northern Greece, the Peloponnese and abroad operate out of Larissa Station, which is accessible by metro. Buses are often faster and cheaper than trains, and operate from Terminal A (100 Kifissou Ave.) to the Peloponnese and western and northern Greece, and from Terminal B (260 Liossion St.) to central and northern Greece.

Boats to and from the Cyclades operate out of Piraeus (accessible by bus and metro). Schedules change daily but can be checked at www.greekferries.gr or www.gtp.gr.

## ▸▸Getting Around

Three metro lines dissect the city and provide access to most major attractions. Suburban and trolley buses run every 15 minutes. Tickets are €1.20 for a single ride or €1.40 a 90-min multiple trip. Tickets must be purchased from a kiosk before boarding the bus.

A three-line tram system connects the city center with the southern coastal area of Athens, running 24hrs on weekends. The tram, bus and metro system operates daily from 5:30am to 1am (2:30am Fri/Sat). Day passes (€4) and week passes (€14) allow unlimited use.

## ▸▸Visitor Info

www.breathtakingathens.com

## ▸▸Quick Facts

**Calling Information**
*Country Code*: 30

*Calling in Greece*: add a "0" before the area code

*Calling overseas*: 00+country code+area code+number

**Currency & Exchange Rates**
*Currency*: Euro (€)

*Currency Breakdown*:
100 cents equals €1

*Exchange Rates*: €1 costs: US$1.30/ £.81/AUD$1.24/ CAN$1.28

## ▸▸Hostels

**Athens Backpackers**
12 Makri Street
(01-922-4044)

**Athens Int'l Hostel (HI)**
16 Victor Hugo Street
(01-523-4170)

**Athens Style**
Agias Theklas N°10 Monastiraki
(01-322-5010)

**Fivos Hostel**
23 Athinas St., Monastiraki
(01-322-6657)

**Hostel Aphrodite**
12 Einardou & 65 Michail Voda Cnr.
*Victoria Square* (01- 881-0589)

**The Student & Travellers Inn**
16 Kydathineon Street, *Plaka*
(01-324-4808)

## ▸▸Things to See & Do

The tourist information office at Tsoha 24 (210-870-7000, www.gnto.gr) provides detailed maps, an indispensable city guide and bus, train and ferry schedules.

The city's biggest draw, the Acropolis, resides atop a hill hovering over the picturesque Plaka district. Don't miss its museum, slightly hidden behind the Parthenon, home to many of the original statues found within. Behind the Acropolis, the ancient city of Agora is a sprawling bed of ruins that include remains of the earliest courtrooms, Senate buildings and law libraries. Just off Amelias St., the Temple of Olympian Zeus lies in ruined, Ozymandius-like glory. You can visit the above three sites, plus two others, for a €12 ticket issued at the Acropolis. Other must-see attractions include the Archaeological Museum, which provides an important overview of Greek history, the Panathenaic Stadium – host to the first modern Olympic games – and Lycabettus Hill, which offers the best views of the city (take the funicular from Aristippou and Ploutarchou Streets for €6).

### ▸▸Day Trips
### Ruins

Delphi – a three-hour, €12.60 bus ride from Athens – lies nestled among gorgeous mountains, and is known as the "navel of the Earth" (ancient Greeks believed that life originated there). Follow the main street 1 km uphill to reach the archaeological site. A ticket is €6 or €9 including the museum. Also, visit the Temple of Poseidon at Cape Sounion, Epidaurus, a well-preserved 4th-century BC theater with excellent acoustics, Ancient Corinth, an impressive ancient city, and Mycenae, the legendary home of the Atreides, set in dramatic cliffs.

### Beaches

The Sardonic Gulf Islands offer beautiful beaches, vehicle-free streets and unique architecture. All are accessible as a day trip; the length of the ferry ride ranges from one hour (Aegina Island) to five hours (Spetses Island). For a cheaper alternative, visit the beaches just outside of Athens. The southern coast of Attica is the most popular; take a bus or tram from Syntagma.

## ▸▸Food & Nightlife

Catch a play or ballet in the 2nd Century AD Theater of Herodeion at the Acropolis. Visit the Thissio area for an array of bars frequented by locals - try ouzo (a licorice-flavored liquor). Cheap kiosks offer delicious souvlaki (lamb and veggies grilled on skewers) and outdoor cafés abound, but for a truly unique food experience, visit the largest daily food market in Athens, between Armodiou and Aristogeitonos on Athenias Street.

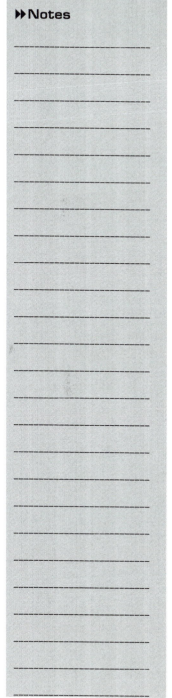

## ▸▸Notes

# ▶Bulgaria

The first thing you need to know about Bulgarians is that they shake their heads for "yes" and nod them for "no" – as if the Cyrillic alphabet isn't confusing enough. But orientation difficulties aside, Bulgaria is a still relatively untouched goldmine of stunning vistas, gorgeous coasts, ancient fortresses and trendy towns filled with friendly, fashionable young people.

## ▶Sofia

In Sofia, upscale boutiques, student bars and McDonalds' arches are perhaps more common than churches and museums, yet the city still retains some of its old world charm. It also serves as a gateway into the nearby mountains, home to the awe-inspiring Rila Monastery and other semi-hidden treasures.

### ▶Getting There

Airport Sofia is a quick bus ride (#84) from the Eagle Bridge, a central landmark. International and domestic trains operate out of Tzentraina Gara – train travel is cheaper, but takes longer than the buses, which arrive to and leave from Sofia's Central Bus Station. Local transportation includes one short metro line in addition to trams, trolleys and buses, which run from 5:30am to 11pm and cost 1 leva or 4 leva for a day ticket (buy a ticket from the kiosk on the street and punch it inside the bus). From the train station, take tram number 12 or 14 to reach the city center. Taxi drivers will smilingly rip off tourists; use only the yellow ones marked with a company name and phone number, and be sure they turn on the meter.

### ▶Things to See & Do

Sofia's sights are centered around Ploshtad Sveta Nedelya. The "yellow street" – Tsar Osvoboditel, Sofia's first paved road – runs north of the square, connecting the Parliament to the gorgeous 1913 St. Nicholas Russian Church and the Royal Palace, which now houses the National Art Gallery and the intriguing National Museum of Ethnography (the Center for Folk Arts and Crafts in its basement is one of the best places to purchase traditional souvenirs). Follow it up past the university to find a free, open garden, ideal for a morning jog or a leisurely afternoon stroll. **Also To See**: The National History Museum, St. Nedelya Cathedra; St. Alexander Nevsky Cathedral.

### ▶Day Trips

Odyssia-In (bul. Stamboliski 20-V, 980-51-02) specializes in hiking trips to Vitosha Mountain, Seven Rila Lakes and other nearby natural wonders

## ▶Visitor Info

www.bulgariatravel.org

## ▶Quick Facts

**Calling Information**
*Country Code*: 359

*Calling in Bulgaria*:
add a "0" before the area code

*Calling overseas*: call the international operator 0023

**Currency & Exchange Rates**
*Currency*: Bulgaria Leva (Leva)

*Exchange Rates*: 1 Leva costs: £.41/US$.66/€.51/AUD$.63/CAN$.65

## ▶Hostels

### ▶Sofia

**Be My Guest Hostel**
13 Ivan Vasov Street
(359-2-989-5092)

**Art Hostel**
21A Angel Kanchev Street
(359-2-980-7898)

**Hostel Mostel**
2 Denkoglu Street
(00359-8-8922-3296)

**Hostel Lavele**
Sofia, 14, Lavele Street
(00359-2-987-23-61)

### ▶Veliko

**Hiker's Hostel**
Rezervoarska 91,
(00359-8-8969-1661)

### ▶Varna

**Yo-Ho Hostel**
bul. Saborni 44
(359-887-933-340)

**Varna Backpackers**
59 Primorski Blvd, apt. 29
(0899472018)

(www.zigzagbg.com). Don't miss an opportunity to visit the must-see Rila Monastery, an enormous, gorgeously painted structure rebuilt in the early 1800s. To get there from Sofia, take tram #5 to the Ovcha Kopel bus station, a bus to Dupnitza, and another to reach the monastery. Leave early, or plan to spend a pleasant, peaceful night in a monastic cell (around 15USD), as the last bus back to Sofia leaves at 3pm. Take an hour-long hike from behind the monastery to visit the shrine of St. Ivan of Rila, the first saint of Bulgaria. Along the way, there's a stone wall where he's said to have lived for six years. Write a wish on a piece of paper and add it to the hopes of others absorbed into its ancient cracks.

## ▸▸Food & Nightlife

For the latest entertainment listings, pick up a free city guide at hotels. Visit opera and theater houses on Rakovski, or chat it up with students at the bars lining the streets of the student district. For a weekly listing of events in English, check out www.programata.bg. And don't miss out on the addictive Shopska salad – an assortment of cucumbers, tomatoes and feta that will give meaning to the Romanian saying, "Don't try to sell cucumbers to the Bulgarian."

## ▸▸Veliko Tarnovo

Set high in the cliffs above the Yantra River, Veliko Tarnovo's windy streets and dramatic cliff-side views rival those of Santorini, Greece or Cinque Terre, Italy. And as if that's not enough, the city's skyline is framed by an enormous fortress on Tsarevets Hill, the ancient capital of the Second Bulgarian Empire. In summer months, a surreal light and sound show floods the sky above it in the early evening hours. About a 5km walk, or cheap taxi ride, from town, the hillside village of Arbanasi is full of cheap restaurants and well-hidden treasures, including the Nativity Church, St. Michael's Gabriel Church and the Konstantsalieva House.

## ▸▸Varna

The sprawling seaside resort of Varna boasts beachfront luxury and shopping galore, all set along the picturesque Black Sea coast. Get lost in the 8 km-long park housing a Dolphinarium, among other attractions, or view the world's oldest gold artifacts at the Archaeology Museum. Take a day trip to Kaliakra, an enormous 13th century fortress, rooted on a cliff from which forty virgins are said to have jumped to their deaths in order to evade the Turks. Or, visit the gorgeous beaches and ruins of Greek Byzantine settlements at the nearby coastal cities of Messembria and Sozopol.

▸▸Notes

_____

_____

_____

_____

_____

_____

_____

_____

_____

_____

_____

_____

_____

_____

_____

_____

_____

_____

_____

_____

_____

_____

_____

_____

_____

_____

_____

# ▸▸Romania

As Romania struggles to leave its oppressive Communist past behind and enter the European Union, the country is at once seeped in tradition and cloaked in modernity. Outside of bustling Bucharest, cars share the road with horse-drawn carts toting freshly farmed cabbage. From the sensory delights of cheap opera and symphony to the castles of Transylvania, home of the legendary Vlad Tepes (model for Bram Stoker's "Dracula"), and the painted monasteries of Bocavina, Romania has much to offer the adventurous tourist.

## ▸▸Bucharest

Romania's rather bleak, grey capital is easily bypassed by those literally in search of greener pastures, but its rich history and fascinating museums make it worth, at the very least, a brief visit.

### ▸▸Getting There

Domestic and international flights arrive at Otopeni Airport, 16 km from the city center. Bus number 783 runs from the airport to Piata Unirii. Trains stop at Gara de Nord, slightly northwest of the city center. City buses cost L1.3 and run until 11:59pm. After hours, take a taxi, but be careful – Romanian cabbies are known to be scam artists. Reputable companies include Cristaxi, Taxi Cobalescu and Taxi 2000. Ask for an approximate price first, and always make sure the meter is running. The price should be L2 base plus L2 per km.

### ▸▸Things to See & Do

Most of Bucharest's sights are located along the length of the main street, which changes its name four times as it runs north-south from Piata Victoriei to Piata Unirii. Begin with a look at rural Romanian life at the Museum of the Romanian Peasant and the open-air Village Museum. Then, head south to the National Art Museum, located to the left of Piata Revolutieri, where the first shots of the 1989 revolution were fired. Stop in for a bejeweled experience at the National History Museum. And finally, head west after crossing the river to ogle at the must-see Parliamentary Palace. Erected by Communist Dictator Nicolae Ceausescu as he demolished much of the city's 19th-century architecture and displaced its population, the building – second in size only to the Pentagon – is as demonstrative of his ego as of his folly.

### ▸▸Food & Nightlife

Pasaj Macca, a tiny alleyway just off Victoriei Street, is a reveler's paradise, resplendent with everything from hookah bars to a Scottish-style, underground pub.

## ▸▸Visitor Info

www.romaniatourism.com

## ▸▸Quick Facts

**Calling Information**
*Country Code*: 40

*Calling in Slovenia*:
add a "0" before the area code

*Calling overseas*: 00+country code+area code+number

**Currency & Exchange Rates**
*Currency*: Romania New Lei (L), coins: 1,10, 50, 100 Bani. 100 bani=1 lei

*Exchange Rates*: 1 Lei (L) costs: £.18/US$.29/€.22/AUD$.27/CAN$.28

## ▸▸Hostels

### ▸▸Bucharest
**Villa Butterfly**
St. Dumitru Zosima 82
(40-747-032-644)

**Funky Chicken Guesthouse**
Str. Gen. Berthelot 63
(40-312-14-25)

### ▸▸Suceava
**Class Hostel**
195 Aurel Vlaicu Street
(40-723-782-328)

### ▸▸Brasov
**Rolling Stone Hostel**
Piatra Mare 2A,
(40-268-513-965)

### ▸▸Sighisoara
**Nathan's Villa Sighisoara**
St. Libertatii 8
(40-265-772-546)

### ▸▸Cluj-Napoca
**Retro Youth Hostel**
Potaissa st. 13
(40-264-450-452)

## ▸▸Suceava

Once the capital of Moldovia, Suceava is now a rather dingy and depressed town. Nevertheless, it offers a spectacular view from the impressive 1388 Citadel of the Throne (follow the stone pathway next to McDonalds in the town center), and provides an ideal jumping-off point to tour the area's legendary painted monasteries, a UNESCO World Heritage Site. Two are within walking distance of the town; to view the others, rent a car or take a worthwhile tour offered by Class Hostel (90 lei plus entrance fees). Travelers can also sleep overnight in the monasteries for a minimal price.

## ▸▸Brasov

The best views of this postcard-worthy town are from the top of Mt. Tampa (a one hour hike or quick cable car ride from the center), although the ancient White and Black Towers across town strive to compete. From September to May, opera and orchestra prices can be had at reasonable prices – pick up a schedule or free city map at the helpful tourist office, housed in the Country History Museum in the central square. Be sure to make the 45-minute excursion to neighboring Bran to view the dramatic "Dracula's Castle," and stop in Rashnov to view an impressive, partially reconstructed castle along the way.

## ▸▸Sighisoara

Known for being the birthplace of Vlad Tepes, the small town is built around a 1911 citadel. At the entrance, a clock tower houses a small torture room and a museum of medieval armory. Eat in the café housed in the building where Tepes toddled, or simply stroll along windy, cobblestone streets. Climb the stairs to a rather creepy cemetery, or tour the surrounding countryside with Eyetours, which provides worthwhile, daylong excursions from Nathan's Villa.

## ▸▸Cluj-Napoca

Trendy Cluj Napoca's bustling shopping district is centered around Piata Unirii, which houses the Museum of Art and the imposing Saint Michael Catholic Church. Second-hand shops are bountiful, as are patisseries, upscale coffee houses and nightclubs (Obsession is considered one of the best in Romania). Check at hotels for up-to-date entertainment listings; ask at Retro Hostel about day trips. For a more accessible respite from the city, take a stroll through the expansive Alexandru Borza Botanical Gardens (5 lei), amid gravestones in the Hazsongardi Cemetery – Transylvania's oldest – or up the hill off Dragalina Street for a fantastic birds-eye view.

## ▸▸Notes

# ▸▸Slovenia

## ▸▸Ljubljana

In Ljubljana travelers can experience the small town "feel" while taking advantage of this capital city's resources, history and culture. Being centrally located in Slovenia it makes for a good base to explore the country's mountains, lakes and caves. Partially on the Mediterranean and linking central Europe to the Balkans, a mix of Italian and Austro-Hungarian influences abound here and around Slovenia.

There are few "must-see" attractions, but it is worth a visit for its lively, youthful energy. Absorb the atmosphere with a stroll through the **Baroque old town** where you will find many quaint cafés along the Ljubljanica river and street performers playing tunes in the main square. The large student population provides for an active nightlife. Some of the hippest clubs have been converted from old army barracks, a reminder of Slovenia's recent past as part of the former Yugoslavia. This is a progressive place with a kind, helpful folk willing to engage in conversation in a multitude of languages.

In July and August student dormitories are open to the public, but during the off-season there are few options for budget accommodation, so book in advance.

### ▸▸Getting There

Slovenia's national air carrier is Adria Airways. Discount airline RyanAir also flies there from its hubs in Trieste, Italy and Klagenfurt, Austria (both are just a short train ride too). From Brnik Airport, bus (lane No. 28), airport shuttle, or taxi will take you the 23km to Ljubljana.

There are a number of buses and trains from Austria, Hungary, Italy and Croatia that all arrive at the same location, Trg Osvobodilne Fronte (Trg OF), which is within walking distance of the center of this compact city. Ferry service from Italy is also available during the high season.

### ▸▸Things to See & Do

There is a **Tourist Information** office inside the train station and also in the Kresija building (Stritarjeva ul 2) by the triple bridge.

### Ljubljanski Grad

The main point of interest is **Castle Hill** and its fortress, **Ljubljana Castle** (€6). A typical medieval city with a castle-crowned hill, this site is the symbol of Ljubljana. Climb the tower and check out the view from above. There is also an interactive museum inside.

### Triple Bridge

At the entrance to the old town, this bridge will bring you to Prešernov Trg. The middle portion was built in 1842 while the two outer sides were added in 1931.

## ▸▸Visitor Info

www.slovenia-tourism.si

## ▸▸Quick Facts

**Calling Information**
*Country Code*: 386

*Calling in Slovenia*:
add a "0" before the area code

*Calling overseas*: 00+country code+area code+number

**Currency & Exchange Rates**
*Currency*: Euro (€)

*Exchange Rates*: €1 costs: US$1.30/ £.81/AUD$1.24/ CAN$1.28

## ▸▸Hostels

### ▸▸Ljubljana
**Bit Center Hotel**
Litijska cesta 57
(1-548-0055)

**Hostel Celica**
Metelkova 8
(1-430-1890)

**Dijaški dom Tabor**
Vidovdanska ul 7; open July and August only (1-232-1067)

**Dijaški Dom Bezigrad**
Kardeljeva pl 28; open July and August only (1-534-2867)

**Villa Veselova**
Veselova ulica 14
(1-599-26721)

### ▸▸Lake Bled
**Bledec Hostel**
Grajska cesta 17
(4-574-5250)

**Int'l Backpackers House Bled**
Selo 11 A Zirovnica
(1-616-889)

### ▸▸Piran
**Val Hostel**
Gregorciceva ul 38a
(5-673-255)

## Ljubljana Walking Tour and Boat Ride

2hr tour includes a walk past the major sights of the old part of Ljubljana and a boat ride along the Ljubljanica river. Apr 1-Oct 31, daily at 2pm (€10). Tour starts from the square in front of the Town Hall (Mestna hiša). Save €1, buy your ticket at the TIC Ljubljana tourist info centre Adamic-Lundrovo nabre•je 2.

### ▶▶Food and Nightlife

Tourist information has several English language guides available, but your best bet is to ask a local about the bars and restaurants.

## ▶▶Lake Bled

The lakeside town of Bled, in the northwest corner of Slovenia, borders the Julian Alps. It's a great stop (possible as a day trip from Ljubljana) for any-one interested in natural beauty and outdoor sports, although it can get crowded and expensive during the summer and winter seasons. There is one lodge-like hostel, camping opportunities and pri-vate accommodation options. A swim or walk around the trout and carp filled glacial lake and a hike to Vintgar gorge are great, cheap activities. There is also an easily accessible hillside castle with far-reaching views. Another activity is a visit by gondola to the lake's tiny island and its church. It is the country's sole island! Getting there from Ljubljana by train is an option; the Bled station is a few kilometers from the town. Regular bus service is a better option and takes about an hour.

## ▶▶Lake Bohinj

A short bus ride (26km) from Bled, this lake is larger and more dramatically alpine. A cable car will take you 1000m up Mt Vogel, making it possible to sum-mit in a couple of hours. Ascents of Slovenia's high-est peak, Mt Triglav (2864m) begin here.

## ▶▶Škocjan Caves

The caves (UNESCO World Heritage listed) are reachable via bus from Ljubljana (1hr) followed by a 45 minute walk. It is their enormous size which makes them a sight to behold. The Postojna caves are a more accessible option in the Karst region, but it is worth the extra effort to get to Škocjan. There are guided tours at both locations.

## ▶▶Piran

If you want a glimpse of Slovenia's short coastline, Piran is the place to go. It is best in summer when fisherman lay their lines off the shore. If coming into the country from Italy, it will be on your way.

### ▶▶Notes

_____
_____
_____
_____
_____
_____
_____
_____
_____
_____
_____
_____
_____
_____
_____
_____
_____
_____
_____
_____
_____
_____
_____
_____
_____
_____
_____
_____
_____

# ▶Croatia

Made up of 6,000 kilometers of coastline, Croatia is a haven for ocean side fun. Dalmatia contains the more popular islands and resorts and is well worth the added time and effort to travel south. Inland, the Plitvice Lakes National Park is a gorgeous sprawl of woods and waters. Skip the capital, Zagreb, if you are headed down the coast, unless a craving for nightlife sets in.

## ▶Dalmatia

With the Adriatic Sea on one side and the Dinaric Alps on the other, the southern part of Croatia from Zadar to Dubrovnik contains some of the Mediterranean's most postcardesque scenery. From untouched green isles to old Venetian fortresses, the coast is a haven for sun, nature and medieval architecture and history. Split, Hvar, Korcula and Dubrovnik are beautiful destinations.

There are hostels in most of the main towns as well as rooms provided by locals. Expect to be greeted aggressively with room offers at the bus stations and boat docks. Agree on a price beforehand and only get in a car if you don't mind staying out of the town center.

### ▶Getting There & Around

Jadrolinija ferry is a beautiful way to get around Dalmatia. You can purchase individual legs or you can buy a one way or round trip journey all the way from the Istrian port of Rijeka to Dubrovnik, which allows for one stopover of up to a week.

## ▶Dubrovnik

Located at the southern tip of Croatia, Dubrovnik is the country's most famous destination. It was heavily bombed in the civil war of the early '90s, but with substantial international aid has rebuilt and regained its splendor. During medieval times Dubrovnik held off Venetian aggression. The testament to this strength is in its powerful city walls. Spend a day exploring the old town or hop the ferry to Lokrum Island to relax in more natural surroundings. For true day trips, look into the Elaphite Islands, Mljet National Park and Cavtat.

### ▶Getting There & Around

Flying from Zagreb to Dubrovnik is a good alternative to the bus which takes 11 hours. From the airport there is the Atlas bus (35 KN) that will take you to the old town or bus station. Ferry is another possibility and, although slow and a bit pricier, any leg of the journey from Split is well worth it for the amazing coastal scenery. The main company is Jadrolinija (www.jadrolinija.hr). There is also a ferry to/from Bari in Italy.

## ▶Visitor Info

www.croatia.hr
www.tzdubrovnik.hr

## ▶Quick Facts

### Calling Information
*Country Code*: 385

*Calling in Croatia*:
add a "0" before the area code

*Calling overseas*: 00+country code+area code+number

### Currency & Exchange Rates
*Currency*: Kuna (KN)

*Exchange Rates*: 1 Kuna costs: £.11/US$.17/€.13/AUD$.16/CAN$.17

## ▶Hostels

### ▶Dubrovnik
**Dubrovnik Youth Hostel**
Ulica bana Jelacica 15-17
(020-232-41)

**YH Dubrovnik**
Vinka Sagrestana 3
(020-423-241)

### ▶Hvar
**Jagoda & Ante Bracanovic Guesthouse**
Šime Buzolica Tome 21
(021-741-416)

### ▶Other Croatia
**Al's Place**
Kruziseva 10, *Split*
(989-182-923)

**Backpackers Fairytale**
Istarska ulica 3 *Split*
(95-824-4894)

**YH Zadar**
Obala Kneza Trpimira 76, *Zadar*
(23-331-145)

**Funk hostel**
Poljicka ulica 13A, *Zagreb*
(01-6314-530)

**YH Zagreb**
Petrinjska street 77, *Zagreb*
(14-841-261)

Buses to the old town operate regularly and are especially helpful if you are staying in the popular Lapad area. The bus ticket is 12KN from a kiosk and 15KN from the driver. The old town is a half hour walk from Lapad.

## ▶▶Things to See & Do

The main tourist info office is just before the Pile Gate entrance to the old town. There is also cheap Internet access on site.

### The Old City Walls

Walk the entire circuit around the old city from the 25m high city walls. They were built and fortified between the 13th and 16th centuries. The protection offered by this structure is astounding. Bring your camera as the different views around each bend all make for excellent photo opportunities. (70KN/30KN, adult/student).

### Mt Srd

The 412 metre summit used to be reachable by cable car. Now the only access is a hike up the switchback trail. It's a moderate walk. Allow an hour from the old town. At the top is a fort built by Napoleon's army in 1808 and which housed discos in the 1980s. It was also the site where the defenders of Dubrovnik made their last stand in the recent war. It is now bullet riddled, decimated and derelict. The panoramic view is absolutely magnificent and above the old town you get a strong sense of the military strength of medieval Dubrovnik.

## ▶▶Split

This is the largest coastal city and a good stopping point before the journey further south. It is a major hub for buses and ferries. The ruins of Diocletian's Palace, built by the Romans in 300 AD, is worth a visit.

## ▶▶Hvar

The narrow cobbled streets and marble old town square are reminiscent of Venice. Take a dip off the rocky beaches or simply suck in the lavender and rosemary scents while you tan. There is a typical Croatian market with fresh eggs and cheeses that make for nice omelets. For activity you can climb to the top of the old town fortress. If motivated to explore, boat taxis will take you to the uninhabited neighboring islands. Adventure seekers with a bit of time and Kuna to burn can take a PADI certification SCUBA course. There are excellent diving opportunities which include explorations of shipwrecks.

## ▶▶Korcula

Korcula boasts the most abundant vegetation in the region and includes olive trees and vineyards which the locals use to make olive oil and wine. In summer there is a weekly Moreška, a fighting dance with swords that has been performed for more than 400 years.

## ▶▶Notes

# ⏭ Bosnia-Herzegovina

Off the beaten path in Bosnia-Herzegovina there is much for the independent backpacker to discover on his/her own. With few must-see attractions, the draw of the country lies in the easily accessible people and incredible natural beauty. It is also serves as a harsh and sorrowful lesson on the effects of war. Travel anywhere by bus and you will see the endless streams of utterly demolished houses. They are striking alongside the gorgeous aqua rivers and grand mountains. Despite the constant historical reminders of violence, Bosnia is a safe place to travel.

## ⏭Sarajevo

Sarajevo rests in the Miljacka River valley and is surrounded by the mountains which were home to the 1984 Winter Olympics. A true link between East and West, its location in the central Balkans has kept Sarajevo in the crosshairs of world history. In 1914 it made global headlines when the Austrian Archduke was assassinated on its street , sparking World War I. There's also a long history of religious tolerance which explains the close proximity of the mosques, synagogues and orthodox and Catholic churches. The recent war in Bosnia devastated the city and its inhabitants, and although the scars are visible in the shell-shocked pavement (referred to as roses) and demolished buildings, the progress is substantial. Much has been rebuilt and streetcars now zip down the road once dubbed "Sniper's Alley," the street where civilians were shot from the hills above.

Although tourism is still in its nascent stage, the spirit and recovery is deeply moving. Sarajevo is famous for its International Film Festival and thrives on culture and the arts. The people are warm and forthcoming and may respectfully approach you with offers of private accommodation.

### ⏭Getting There

Bus is the most common form of transport into and out of Sarajevo. There are many routes from Croatia and regular service to Belgrade. There is also daily train service to Zagreb and an overnighter to Budapest. The bus and train station are located next to each other on the west side.

### ⏭Getting Around

There are trams that run east-west and the No 4 will take you due east to Bašcaršija. The ticket is 1.60 KM at kiosk and 1.80 KM from driver. A day-ticket costs 5.30 KM and can only be bought at the kiosk.

## ⏭Visitor Info

**Visitor Information**
www.bhtourism.ba

## ⏭Quick Facts

**Calling Information**
*Country Code*: 387

*Calling in Bosnia-Herzegovina*: add a "0" before the area code

*Calling overseas*: 00+country code+area code+number

**Currency & Exchange Rates**
*Currency*: Convertible Mark (KM)

*Exchange Rates*: 1 KM costs: £.41/US$.66/€.51/AUD$.63/CAN$.65

## ⏭Hostels

### ⏭Sarajevo
**Sartour**
M.M. Baseskije 63/3
(33-238-680)

**Hostel Gonzo**
Gatacka 33
(062-476-333)

**Hostel Konak International**
Mula Mustafe Baseskije 48
(33-445-200)

**Hostel Ljubicica Mula Mustafe**
Baeskije 65
(33-535-829)

### ⏭Mostar
**Omar Lakiše**
Mladena Balorde 21A
(0-36-551-627)

**Pansion Most**
Adema Buca 100
(0-36-552-528)

## ▶Accommodation

There is no shortage of private accommodation. All tourism offices have rooms to rent. Pensions and hostels are the budget alternative (although not cheap). Ask around as the burgeoning tourist industry is still being defined.

## ▶Things to See & Do

The tourist office is located at Zelenih Beretki 22. There are also a number of information offices (denoted with i) on Mula Mustafe Bašekija each with tour and accommodation options. Competition is stiff and you should expect to receive only their proprietary options.

### Bašcaršija

The old Turkish quarter with its cobbled streets and pigeon square is full of cafés, eateries and shops. Here you can try authentic Turkish coffee brewed in brass pots, guaranteed to feel like rocket fuel, or sample the greasy burek meat pastries.

### The War Tunnel Museum

Located near the airport, a guided tour is the easiest way to visit this small museum. During the Serbian siege of Sarajevo from 1992-1995, the only way in and out of the city was through the 800 meter tunnel dug underneath the airport. There is a small uncollapsed section of the tunnel and a room of relics and reading material. (5 KM).

### The Eternal Flame

On Mula Mustafe Bašekija, this flame pays tribute to the victims of World War II. There is talk about expanding the memorial to honor those of the recent war.

## ▶Food & Nightlife

The National Theatre has concerts, ballets and other shows with reasonably priced tickets. The current schedule is available at the tourist office. The bar scene is not fully developed, but on the weekends everyone heads out in droves. City Pub on Zelenih Beretki is always crowded.

## ▶Mostar

Located three hours by regular bus service from Sarajevo, this is a good choice if you are interested in Bosnia-Herzegovina beyond the capital. Visually it is more appealing than Sarajevo. The gorgeous green Neretva River runs through the medieval town valley. The old town is cute and although destroyed in the war, Stari Most, or the old bridge, will be functional again. There are several Turkish Houses which depict life during Ottoman times.

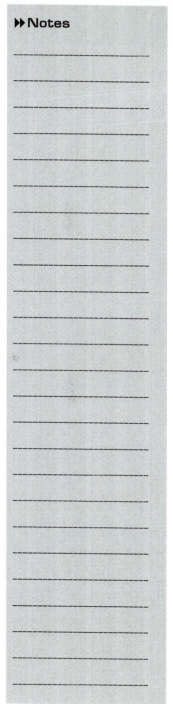

## ▶Notes

# ▶▶Poland

After struggling through a rough 20th century marred by occupation and war, Poland has come back with full force and gained acceptance into the European Union. The main cities of Warsaw and Krakow are rife with regal history and modern culture. There is also a great deal for the outdoorsy types around the awe-inspiring glazed peaks of the Tatra Mountains. However, the very best reason to visit Poland may be its national drink, vodka, which is made in a wide assortment of fruity flavors.

## ▶▶Kraków

Kraków is the most visited city in Poland and for good reasons. Boasting the largest medieval square in all of Europe, the old town shines with historic majesty and a nightlife that pumps into the morning hours. Spared from the destruction of World War II, you may notice the authentic old world feel. A visit to the city is incomplete without a walk around the infamous Jewish quarter of Kazimierz, once home to 65,000 Jewish residents and now less than 200. Get a taste for Polish cuisine with borsch (soup made from beets) and pierogis (like raviolis) - those with a cholesterol conscience beware!

Kraków's location in the southern part of the country makes it an easy stopover between Prague and Budapest on the Eastern European wiggle path. Auschwitz is a day trip and although gut wrenching, it is not to be missed!

### ▶▶Getting There
The Polish airline LOT offers domestic flights from Warsaw, as well as a few other cities in Europe, although the rail network is quite good. The train from Warsaw is 4 hours. For international travel, overnight trains from Budapest, Prague, and Berlin are convenient. Pay close attention to your belongings and heed the safety warnings of other travelers without being overly concerned. Know that it is also possible to travel these routes by day, even if there is no direct service.

All buses, trains, and minibuses arrive and depart from stations near each other at the northern end of the city.

### ▶▶Getting Around
There are trams, but the city is compact and the old town and Kazimierz are best traveled on foot. If upon arrival you want to take the tram to your accommodation, ask at tourist information at the train station.

### ▶▶Things to See & Do
#### Wawel Hill
For 500 years this was the home of the king. Even after central power moved to Warsaw, it still remained the symbol of Poland. A whole morning can be spent ex-

## ▶▶Visitor Info
www.poland.travel

## ▶▶Quick Facts
**Calling Information**
*Country Code*: 48

*Calling in Poland*:
add a "0" before the area code

*Calling overseas*: 00+country code+area code+number

**Currency & Exchange Rates**
*Currency*: Zloty (PLN)

*Exchange Rates*: 1 PLN costs: £.20/ US$.31/€.24/AUD$.30/CAN$.31

## ▶▶Hostels
**Atlantis Hostel**
Dietla 58, *Kraków*
(012-376-7063)

**Dizzy Daisy Hostel**
Pedzichów 9, *Kraków*
(012-376-7064)

**Hostel Rynek7**
Rynek Glówny 7/6, *Kraków*
(012-431-1698)

**Pink Panther's Hostel**
Sw. Tomasza 8, *Kraków*
(012-422-0935)

**Chillout Hostel**
ul. Poznanska 7/7, *Warsaw*
(022-409-98-81)

**Hostel Oki Doki**
Plac Jana Henryka Dabrowskiego 3, *Warsaw*. (022-828-01-22)

**Tamka Hostel**
Tamka 30, *Warsaw*
(022-205-00-42)

**The Warsaw Hostel**
Kopernika 30 Street, *Warsaw*
(022-115-44-42)

ploring the castle, cathedral and exhibits, but a short walk around the grounds is sufficient if you lack the time, interest or funds. The view is free and provides a nice look along the Vistula River. The attractions get crowded, so come early for tickets to the sites.

## Kazimierz

An independent town until the 1800s, Kazimierz once housed a large Jewish community. It became world famous when Steven Spielberg filmed parts of Schindler's List here and depicted the harrowing plight of Poland's Jewish population. The Old Synagogue and its Jewish Museum is just one of the stops possible on a self-guided or organized walking tour. At night there is an emergent energy radiating from the trendy bars and cafés.

## Wieliczka Salt Mine

Described as cheesy and tacky by some and fascinating and mind blowing by others, judge for yourself with a visit. The two-hour guided tour is obligatory and will take you underground to view the carvings, statues and rooms, all scratched from salt. Ancient and modern mining techniques are also explained. There are minibuses that depart regularly from the bus station for the 15 minute ride. (73 PLN tour fee).

## Ⓕ Auschwitz and Birkenau

The most notorious of all the concentration camps and perhaps the very symbol for genocide in the 20th century, both sites can be seen in a day. Admission is free. A 15-minute documentary film from the liberation is a good start to the visit, after which you can explore the grounds. There is an excellent 3.5 hour tour for 250 PLN or, if you go unguided, the pamphlet "Auschwitz Birkenau Guide Book" is recommended. Birkenau is 3km from Auschwitz and is even more devastating in its vastness and incomprehensible capacity for human extermination. Minibuses depart from a fenced in area near the bus station and take two hours. It is suggested that you eat a big breakfast as it will probably be your only meal of the day.

## ▶▶The Tatra Mountains

Shared with Slovakia, the Tatra Mountains (part of the Carpathian range) on the Polish side are two and a half hours south of Kraków. They provide awesome relief from the flatness of Poland's plains and emotionally draining historical cities. Zakopane is the main alpine town and is a top destination for vacationing Poles. There are outstanding hiking opportunities nearby and several PTTK lodge/hostels that provide basic accommodation. The cable car to Mt Kasprowy Wierch and a walk to Lake Morskie Oko are two of the more popular excursions. Private bus companies make regular journeys on the Kraków-Zakopane route. Seat reservations are recommended in the summer and on weekends.

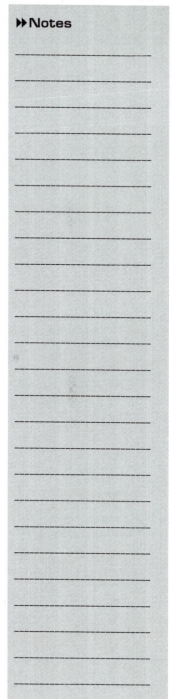

### ▶▶Notes

_____
_____
_____
_____
_____
_____
_____
_____
_____
_____
_____
_____
_____
_____
_____
_____
_____
_____
_____
_____
_____
_____
_____
_____
_____

# ▶▶Baltics

If you're seeking the spirit of a new frontier, head for the Baltic region—it won't be a secret for long. Estonia and Latvia both re-emerged from behind the Soviet Iron Curtain as independent nations in 1991, and have only recently joined the EU. Back on the European map and relatively undiscovered, the picturesque Baltic cities still retain the old-world feel of Prague without the hordes of tourists, while a youthful energy spices up the central squares – cafés, bars and clubs are springing up everywhere. You'll also find a wealth of proud, beautiful architecture remarkably unscathed by war – Estonia's capital, Tallinn, has a medieval old town unrivaled by any in Europe, while Riga, Latvia still holds magnificent Art Nouveau apartment buildings from the golden age of the '30s.

For a change of pace, the naturally flat, lush countryside makes the Baltic region a popular place for bike touring, and the tree-lined seaside, once the favored vacation spot of well-to-do Russians, offers miles of natural beauty. As the new gateway linking Scandinavia to the rest of Eastern Europe, the Baltic region holds many unique and unprecedented delights.

## ▶Tallinn, Estonia

Estonia's miraculous capital is bound to inspire awe. It's an exciting, thriving center that has recently emerged from Soviet occupation, with many breathtaking Gothic buildings that have somehow escaped war damage. Tallinn's Old Town is one of the last remaining truly medieval cities in Europe, with subterranean bars that serve locally-made vodka and absinthe and cast an enticing glow from their stone doorways. You can walk the dozens of winding, cobbled streets within the high wall and ramparts, and then stop for a cheap sandwich made on native thin, dense black bread at one of the many cafés, or "kohviks." Still relatively undiscovered by visitors outside of the EU, this port city is becoming a weekend destination for many of its neighboring countries. It's just a 45-minute ferry ride from Helsinki, a quick train trip from St. Petersburg and is easily accessible from Sweden and Germany.

### ▶Getting There
#### From the airport
Tallinn's pristine, small but modern airport is only 3 km from the city center. Bus #2 leaves from just outside the departures area every 20 minutes and costs the equivalent of less than a dollar; it stops at the Sokos Hotel Viru in the city center and also right next to the old town.

## ▶Visitor Info
Estonia - www.visitestonia.com
Latvia - www.latviatourism.lv

## ▶Quick Facts
**Calling Information**
*Country Code*:
372 Estonia, 371 Latvia

*Calling overseas*: 00+country code+area code+number

**Currency & Exchange Rates**
*Currency*: Estonia is the Euro; Latvia is the Latvian Lati (LVL)

*Exchange Rates*: €1 costs: US$1.30/ £.81/AUD$1.24/ CAN$1.28

*Exchange Rates*: 1 LVL costs: £1.16/ US$1.86/€1.44/AUD$1.77/CAN$1.83

## ▶Hostels
### ▶Tallinn, Estonia
**Baltic Backpackers**
Uus 14. *Old Town*
(517-1337)

**Hostel Vana Tom**
Väike-Karja 1, *Old Town*
(631-3252)

**Mahtra Hostel**
Mahtra 44
(621-8828)

### ▶Tartu, Estonia
**Hostel Student Village**
Narva 25
(740-9955)

**Herne B&B**
Herne 59
(744-1959)

**Tähtvere**
Laulupeo 19
(742-1708)

## Rail

The train station is directly across the street from the old city; to get there, just walk through the underpass across the main Rannamäe tee road and head up Nunne Street.

## Ferry

The high-tech, ever-expanding ferry terminal is just three or four blocks' walking distance from the old city. Alternatively, buses #92 and 90 can take you from Terminal D to the heart of the city center.

## Long-Distance Bus

Buses serve all major towns and are generally cheaper, more frequent and faster than the train. Eurolines leaves from the bus station at Lastekodu 46, 1km from downtown. Buses also go from here to major cities in Russia, Poland and Germany. www.eurolines.ee.

## ▸Getting Around
## Public Bus and Tram System

Most of the city is easily explored on foot. Buses and trams tend to get crowded, but the public transit system is functional and serves all entry points to the city. Tickets are sold at kiosks for €1 a ride or from the driver for €1.60. Newsstands also sell 1hr (€1.20), 1-day (€4) and 3-day tickets (€6). Most transport ends at midnight. The Tallinn Card offers free public transport as well as admission to 40 museums/sights and a free 2 ½ hour tour. Cost is 6hrs (€12), 24hrs (€24), 48hrs (€ 32) or 72hrs (€40).

## ▸Food & Nightlife

Pick up a copy of *Tallinn This Week*, which lists bars, clubs, restaurants and events. There is also an English-language Baltic City Paper that comes out every two months.

## ▸Tartu, Estonia

Estonia's second largest city is a colorful university hub brimming with culture. Estonians have a name for its vitality -- Tartu vaim, or "Tartu spirit." A stroll though the city takes you through leafy, wooded parks, over pedestrian bridges, and through ruins. You'll find wine bars and beer terraces tucked into old subterranean armories and spontaneous music can be heard from art students on Rüütli Street, off the beaten path. Estonia's National Museum is here (free on Fridays), and from the Stone Bridge over the Emajogi River, the tops of red and yellow Art Nouveau buildings resemble layer cakes with ornate plaster "frosting" accents. At night it's

## ▸Hostels Con't

### ▸Saaremaa Is., Estonia
**Valsi Hostel**
Kastani 20, *Kuressaare*
(45-27-100)

**Saaremaa School Hostel**
Hariduse 13, *Kuressaare*
(52-042)

### ▸Riga, Latvia
**Amber Hostel**
10C Reznas Street
(887-5749)

**Argonaut Hostel**
Kaleju Street 50
(614-7214)

**Elizabeth's Youth Hostel**
Elizabetes iela 101
(955-2184)

**Old Town Hostel**
Kaleju iela 50
(614-7214)

**Posh Backpackers**
Pupolu 5 (Central Market)
(602-0808)

**Riga Backpackers Hostel**
6 Marstelu Street
(722-9922)

### ▸Kuldiga, Latvia
**Ventas Rumba**
Stendes iela
(332-4168)

## ▸Notes

_____
_____
_____
_____
_____
_____
_____
_____
_____
_____

easy to find local live music, popular nightclubs, and fun, campy student hangouts. Pick up a copy of *Tartu This Week* for listings. **To see/do**: Gunpowder Wine Cellar pub, literary cafés, walking trails.

## ►Saaremaa Island, Estonia

Saaremaa, Estonia's largest island just two hours southwest of Tallinn, provides a peaceful, idyllic overnight retreat on the way to Latvia. Buses leave frequently from the mainland and board the ferry for Kuressaare (the main town), where lively taverns, cafés and fresh-air markets draw Estonians and foreigners alike. Rent a bike to tour the green, scenic island with its castles, churches and Dutch-style windmills, climb the defense tower of Kuressaare's 14th-century castle for a view of the Baltic Sea, or row a boat in the moat that surrounds it. **To see/do**: Kuressaare Episcopal Castle, Angla Windmills, traditional Estonian food, Saaremaa vodka.

## ►Riga, Latvia

Riga is a genuinely beautiful old capital that is just waking up and reinventing itself. With one of the finest collections of Jugendstil (Art Nouveau) buildings anywhere in the world, Riga is a feast for the eyes and exhilarating to explore on foot. The movement's eclecticism shows in ornate tiled entrances, smooth-faced giant modern gargoyles, and stained glass in intricately webbed ironwork. Along these museum-like streets, you'll find a mix of the old and the new, from headscarved women selling bunches of flowers to younger urbanites congregating among the beer terraces, cafés and late-night clubs. Smart and cosmopolitan, Riga is quickly working to regain its 1930s reputation as the "Paris of the Baltics."

### ►Getting There
#### From the airport
The airport is 8 km southwest of the city. Bus # 22 departs from Abrenes Street for the city center (Strelnieku laukums and the train station) every 10-30 minutes and costs 0.70Ls, while express bus # 22A leaves on an erratic schedule for the Orthodox Cathedral and costs 0.70Ls. Alternatively, a taxi to the city center costs 8-10Ls.

#### Rail
The train station is right beside Old Riga. Turn left when leaving the station and head toward the black spire of St. Peter's Church, then walk through the

## ►Notes

underpass and follow the signs for 13.janvara iela and turn right onto Aspazijas bulvaris.

### Ferry
The ferry terminal and yacht harbor lie less than 1km north of Old Riga. Take trams # 7, 5 or 9 from Ausekla two stops to the city center.

### Long-Distance Bus
Tram #7 stops in front of the bus terminal; ride it one stop further into the center (0.40Ls). To get there on foot, turn left, walk under the underpass into the tunnel and follow the signs for Vecriga-Valnu iela into Old Riga.

## ▶Getting Around
### Public Bus and Tram System
Riga has 11 tram lines, 20 trolleybus routes and 52 bus routes, which run from 05:30-23:30. A ride anywhere in the city costs a flat 0.5Ls, a day card is 1.90Ls. The Riga Card provides free use of trams and trolleybuses and free admission/discounts at museums and is available for 24, 48, or 72 hours (12/14/18Ls).

### Long-Distance Bus
Buses serve all major Baltic towns and are generally cheaper, more frequent and faster than the train. Ecolines, Eurolines and Nordeka all leave from the main bus station (autoosta).

## ▶Food & Nightlife
Pick up a copy of the English-language Riga In Your Pocket, which gives frank, fun reviews of bars, clubs and cafés.

## ▶Kuldiga, Latvia
The lush, green medieval town of Kuldiga is located about 2 hours west of Riga by bus. It boasts a 13th century castle surrounded by a moat and the widest natural waterfall in Europe, beneath which people row boats and catch fish with their hands. Nightlife is focused around the canal streets and the many beer gardens set over the water. Head to the popular waterfall hostel, Ventas Rumba, where backpackers hang out.

## ▶Sigulda, Latvia
At the edge of Latvia's Gauja National Park lies Sigulda, famous for its Turaida Stone Castle, mysterious legends, and red sandstone Gûtmanala caves with graffiti dating back to the 1870s. Catch the cable car ride for a great view of the Gauja valley, then hike back through these sights into town. After sunset, backpackers gather at the pizzerias, cafés and bars in the town center.

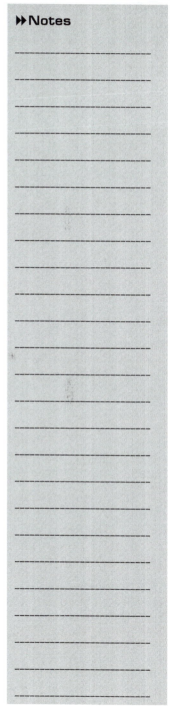

## ▶Notes

# ▸▸Scandinavia

## ▸▸Denmark

### ▸▸Copenhagen

Copenhagen, the epicenter of Denmark and much of Scandinavia, is a fun, lively cultural city that's largely affordable. Small and manageable, there is nothing imposing, nothing overwhelming - you can easily explore on foot its many museums, castles and ancient structures. Walk through charming cobblestone streets, bike ride along the lake, enjoy lunch in a charming restaurant. As English is spoken everywhere, it won't be hard to meet the friendly and well-mannered Danes, especially if there's liquor involved. A young thriving city, take advantage of Copenhagen's liberal vibe, exhibited in the many cafés, bars and never-ending nightclubs. **To See/Do**: National Museet, Tivoli Gardens, Nyhavn, Christiania.

## ▸▸Sweden

### ▸▸Stockholm

Built on islands amidst Lake Mälaren and stretching into the Baltic Sea, Stockholm is one of Europe's most beautiful cities. A blend of well preserved medieval structures and contemporary architecture makes it a city that offers a little bit of everything. There are buses, ferries, subways and bridges that link the different islands, but walking or bicycling around is the best way to get a true feel of this unique coastal city. There is a large young, liberal artistic population and many galleries, bars, cafés and clubs to accommodate. Purchase a Stockholm Card for unlimited access to public transport and free/discounted entry to many attractions. **To See/Do**: Culture House, Museum of Modern Art, archipelago cruise, Rosendall's Gardens.

### ▸▸Gothenburg

While not on the cosmopolitan scale of Stockholm, the west coast city of Gothenburg (Göteborg) has its own distinct identity as a highly artistic and bohemian cultural center. Residents are uncommonly proud of their city and keen to show it off: you'll be surprised at the vast number of design and photography museums and exhibits, theaters, and artsy districts that are enthu-

## ▸▸Visitor Info

**Denmark:**
www.dt.dk

**Finland:**
www.finland-tourism.com

**Norway:**
www.visitnorway.com

**Sweden:**
www.sverigeturism.se

## ▸▸Quick Facts

**Calling Information**

*Country Code*: Denmark 45, Finland 358, Sweden 46, Norway 47

*Calling from within*: add a "0" before the area code

*Calling overseas*: 00+country code+area code+number

**Currency & Exchange Rates**

*Currency*: Finland - Euro (€), Denmark - Krone, Sweden - Krona, Norway - Kroner

*Exchange Rates*: €1 costs: US$1.30/£.81/AUD$1.24/CAN$1.28

1 Danish Krone costs: US$.17/£.11/AUD$.16/CAN$.17/€.13

1 Swedish Krona costs: US$.15/£.09/AUD$.14/CAN$.15/€.12

1 Norwegian Kroner costs: US$.18/£.11/AUD$.17/CAN$.17/€.13

siastically supported by locals. The Opera House, by the railway station, is a fascinating example of contemporary design. The Haga district, along Linnégatan and Vasastan, is a lively student area with an eclectic blend of cafés, secondhand shops, goldsmiths and glasswork studios. The spice merchants and coffee roasters there are reminiscent of its days in the 18th and 19th centuries as a busy trading port. Thrill seekers won't want to miss the largest wooden roller coaster in Scandinavia at the Liseberg amusement park in the city center. **To see/do**: the Haga district, Röhss design museum, the Hasselblad Center (photography).

## ▶Finland

### ▶Helsinki

The most eastern of the major Scandinavian cities (near Russia), Finland's capital, with its remarkable 19th century neoclassical architecture, is another manageable city with a distinctly Eastern European flair. Helsinki's character is very much dominated by the Baltic Sea as there are many bridges and ferries linking the capital to nearby islands. The many cafés, bars, museums, tours and even spas are easily explored on foot. A huge money saver is the **Helsinki Card**, which gives free and/or discounted entry to many attractions and tours, and unlimited access to public transportation. **To See/Do**: Museum of Contemporary Art, Market Square, Senate Square, Suomenlinna (an island), enjoy a day spa.

## ▶Norway

### ▶Oslo

Surrounded by mountains and comprised of beautiful parks, wide streets and pretty harbors, the capital of Norway is a pleasant stop if you're traveling through Scandinavia. A combination of medieval, 19th century neoclassical and 20th century contemporary architecture lends to the developing character of this ancient city. With increasing cultural and nightlife activities, and picturesque scenery, especially in the nearby pastoral communities, it is a pleasant and often interesting stop. **To See/Do**: Edvard Munch Museum, Norwegian Folk Museum, Akershus Castle.

## ▶Hostels

### ▶Copenhagen, Dmk
**City Public Hostel**
**Copenhagen Sleep-In**
Blegdamsvej 132 *(June-Aug)*
(35-26-50-59)

**Danhostel Copenhagen Amager (HI)**
Vejlandsallé 200
(32-52-29-08)

**Danhostel Copenhagen Bellahøj (HI)**
Herbergvejen 8
(38-28-97-15)

**Generator Hostel**
Adelgade 5-7
(45-3369-0505)

**Sleep-In Green**
Ravnsborggade 18
(35-37-77-77)

**Sleep-In Heaven**
Struenseegade 7
(35-35-4648)

### ▶Stockholm, Sweden
**af Chapman & Skeppsholmen**
Flaggmansvägen 8
(08-463-22-66)

**Backpackers Inn (HI)**
Banérgartan 56
(08-660-75-15)

**City BackPackers Hostel**
Upplandsgatan 2a
(08-20-69-20)

**Långholmens Youth Hostel (HI)**
Långholmsmuren 20
(08-668-05-10)

**(HI)**
Zinkens väg 20
(08-616-81-00)

### ▶Helsinki, Finland
**Eurohostel (HI)**
Linnankatu 9
(09-622-0470)

**Stadion Hostel (HI)**
Pohjoinen Stadiontie 3b
(09-477-8480)

### ▶Oslo, Norway
**Anker Hostel**
Storgata 55
(22-997-200)

**Oslo Hostel Haraldsheim (HI)**
Haraldsheimvn 4
(22-22-29-65)

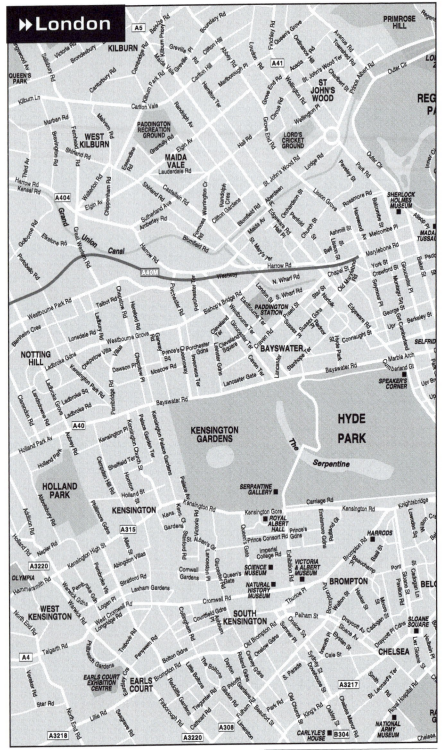

# London

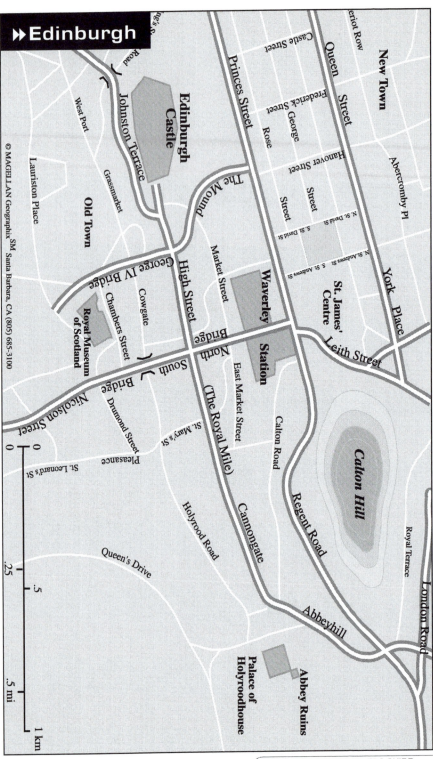

# ►Edinburgh

New Town

Queen Street

Princes Street

Castle Street
Frederick Street
George Street
Rose Street
Hanover Street
N. St. David St
S. St. David St
N. St. Andrews St
S. St. Andrews St

eriot Row

Abercromby Pl

York Place

West Port

Johnston Terrace

Edinburgh Castle

The Mound

Lauriston Place

Grassmarket

Old Town

George IV Bridge

High Street

Market Street

Waverley Station

St. James' Centre

Leith Street

Royal Museum of Scotland

Chambers Street

Cowgate

North Bridge

South Bridge

East Market Street

Calton Road

Calton Hill

Nicolson Street

Drumond Street

Pleasance

St. Leonard's St

St. Mary's St

(The Royal Mile)

Cannongate

Holyrood Road

Regent Road

Royal Terrace

London Road

Queen's Drive

Abbeyhill

Palace of Holyroodhouse

Abbey Ruins

© MAGELLAN Geographix SM Santa Barbara, CA (805) 685-3100

0    .25    .5

0    .5    1 km

.5 mi

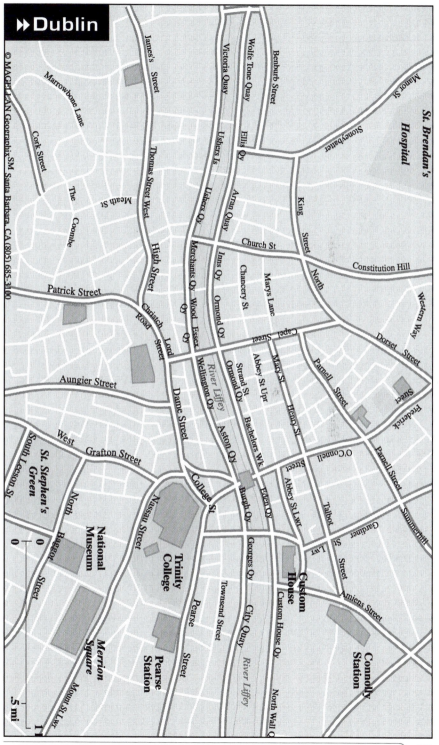

# ▶ Dublin

© MAGELLAN Geographix℠ Santa Barbara, CA (805) 685-3100

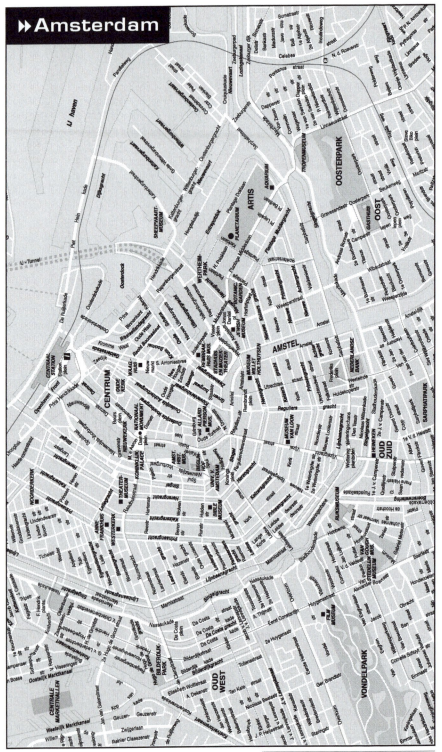

# ▸Amsterdam

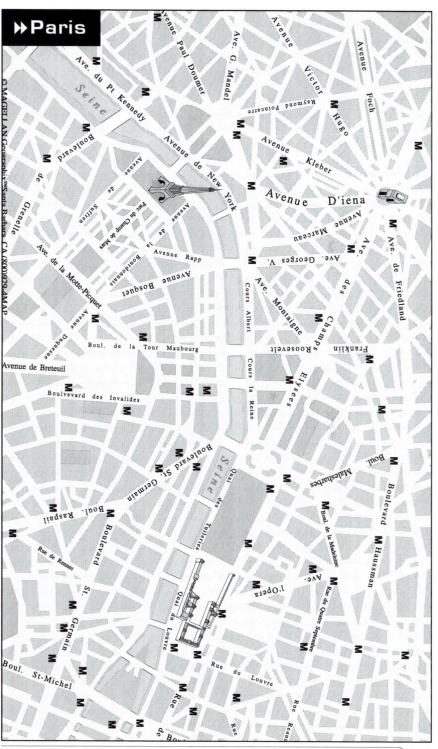

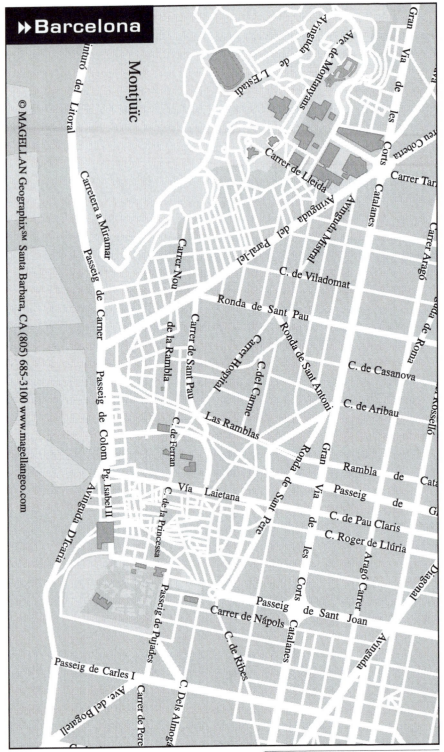

# ▶ Barcelona

Montjuïc

© MAGELLAN Geographix℠ Santa Barbara, CA (805) 685-3100 www.magellango.com

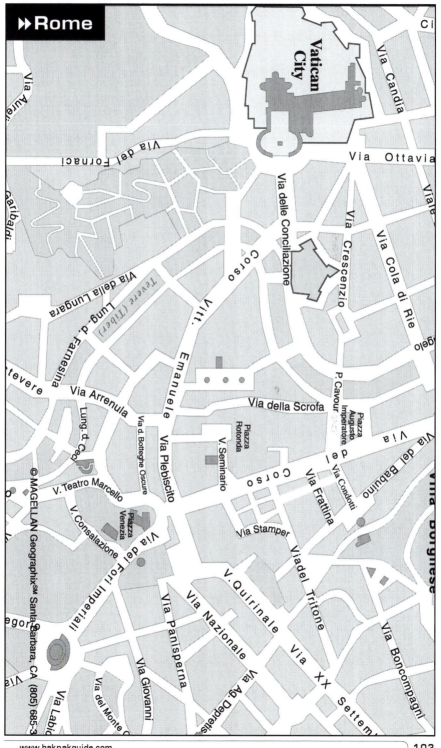

# ►Rome

Vatican City

Via Candia

Via Ottavia

Viale

Via del Fornaci

Via della Conciliazione

Corso

Via Crescenzio

Via Cola di Rie

Vitt.

Corso

Via della Lungara

Tevere (Tiber)

Lung. d.

Via Farnesina

Emanuele

Via Arrenula

Via della Scrofa

Piazza Augusto Imperatore

Via del Babuino

Lung. d. Ceo

Via d. Botteghe Oscure

Via Plebiscito

Piazza Rotonda

V. Seminario

Corso

Via Frattina

Via Condoti

Via

Villa Borghese

V. Teatro Marcello

V. Consalazione

Piazza Venezia

Via dei Forii Imperiali

Via Stamper

Via del Tritone

Via Boncompagni

V. Quirinale

Via Nazionale

Via XX Settem...

Via Panisperna

Via Ag. Depretis

Via Giovanni

Via del Monte C...

Via Labi...

© MAGELLAN Geographix℠ Santa Barbara, CA (805) 685-3...

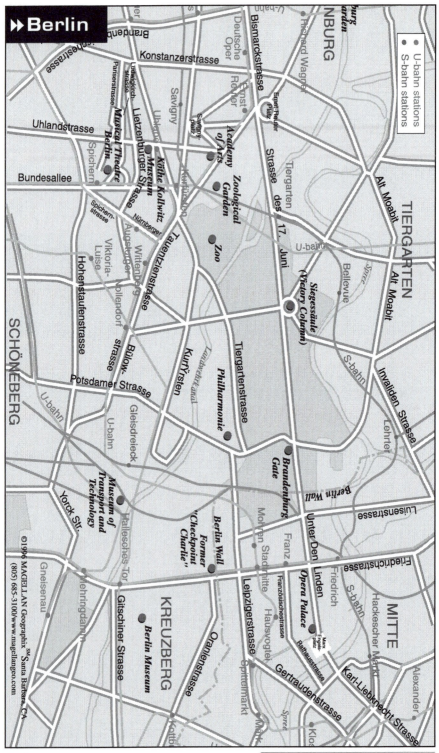

# ⏩ Berlin

U-bahn stations
S-bahn stations

NBURG

TIERGARTEN

SCHÖNEBERG

KREUZBERG

MITTE

Konstanzerstrasse
Bismarckstrasse
Deutsche Oper
Brandenburg
Richard Wagner
burg garden

Uhlandstrasse
Ludwigkirch-strasse
Pariserstrasse
Musical Theatre Berlin
Uhland
Savigny
Ernst Reuter Platz
Ernst Reuter Strasse

Bundesallee
Spichern
Lietzenburger Strasse
Käthe Kollwitz Museum
Nürnberger
Academy of Arts
Zoological Garden
Zoo
Strasse des 17. Juni
Tiergarten
U-bahn
Bellevue
Spree
Alt Moabit
Alt Moabit

Spichern-strasse
Viktoria-Luise
Augsburger
Wittenberg
Tauenzienstrasse
Kurfürsten
Siegessäule (Victory Column)
Invaliden Strasse
Lehrter

Hohenstaufenstrasse
Bollendorf strasse
Bülow-
Landwehrkanal
Kurfürsten
Tiergartenstrasse
Philharmonie
S-bahn

Potsdamer Strasse
U-bahn
Gleisdreieck
U-bahn
Brandenburg Gate
Berlin Wall
Luisenstrasse

Yorck Str.
Museum of Transport and Technology
Hallesches Tor
Berlin Wall Former "Checkpoint Charlie"
Mohren
Franz
Unter Den Linden
Stadtmitte
Französischestrasse
Hausvogtei
Friedrichstrasse
Friedrich
S-bahn
Hackescher Markt
Alexander

Gneisenau
Mehringdamm
Mehringdamm
Gitschiner Strasse
Berlin Museum
KREUZBERG
Oranienstrasse
Leipzigerstrasse
Spittelmarkt
Opera Palace
Rathausstrasse
Marx Public Platz
Gertraudenstrasse
Karl-Liebknecht Strasse
Spree
Klos...

©1996 MAGELLAN Geographix℠Santa Barbara, CA
(805) 685-3100/www.magellango.com

Kottb...
Spree
Mark...

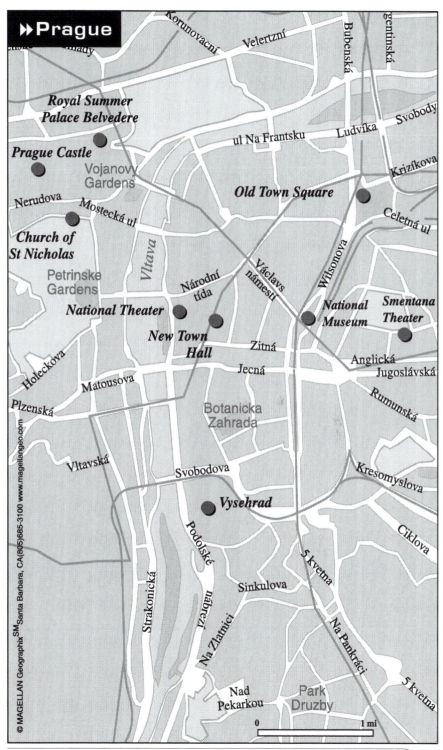

# ▶Prague

Korunovacní
Velertzní
Bubenská
gentinská

Royal Summer
Palace Belvedere

Svobody

ul Na Frantsku
Ludvíka

Prague Castle

Krizíkova

Vojanov
Gardens

Old Town Square

Celetná ul

Nerudova

Mostecká ul

Church of
St Nicholas

Vltava

Petrinske
Gardens

Národní
tída

Václavs
námestí

Wilsonova

National Theater

National
Museum

Smentana
Theater

New Town
Hall

Zitná

Anglická
Jugoslávská

Jecná

Holeckova

Matousova

Rumunská

Plzenská

Botanicka
Zahrada

Vltavská

Svobodova

Kresomyslova

Vysehrad

Ciklova

Strakonická

Podolské nábrezí

5 kvetna

Sinkulova

Na Pankráci

Na Zlatnici

Nad
Pekarkou

Park
Druzby

5 kvetna

0          1 mi

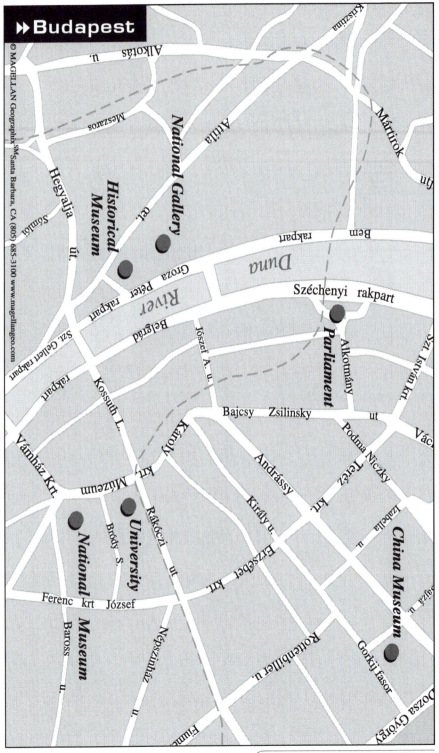

▶ Budapest

© MAGELLAN Geographix℠ Santa Barbara, CA (805) 685-3100 www.magellangeo.com

Alkotás u.

Mészáros

Mártírok utja

National Gallery

Attila

Hegyalja út

Historical Museum

Somlói

ot.

Groza Péter rakpart

River

Bem

rakpart

Duna

Széchenyi rakpart

Parliament

Alkotmány

Szt. István krt.

Szt. Gellert rakpart

rakpart

Belgrád

Jószef A. u.

Kossuth L.

Bajcsy Zsilinsky ut

Vác

Vámház Krt.

Károly krt.

Múzeum

Podma Niczky

Teréz

Izabella u

Andrássy

Király u.

Váci

University

Rákóczi ut

Bródy S.

Erzsébet krt.

China Museum

National Museum

Ferenc krt József

Baross u.

Népszínház u

Rottenbiller u.

Gorkij fasor

Fiumei u

Dózsa György

# ▸Useful Phrases

| ▸English | ▸Spanish | ▸German | ▸French |
|---|---|---|---|
| Good Morning | Buenos días | Guten Morgen | Bonjour! |
| Good Evening | Buenas tardes | Guten Abend | Bonsoir! |
| Please | Por Favor | Bitte schön | S'il vous plaît |
| Thank You | Gracias | Danke schön | Merci! |
| Is this the right bus to_____? | ¿Es este el autocar que va a _____? | Ist dies der Bus nach _____? | Est-ce bien l'autocar pour _____? |
| I would like a bus ticket to ____ | Quiero un boleto de autocar para _____ | Ich hätte gerne eine Busfahrkarte nach_ | Un billet pour ____ s'il vous plaît |
| What time does the bus to ___ depart? | ¿A que hora sale el autobús para ___? | Wann fåhrt der Bus nach _____ ab? | Quelle est l'heure de départ de l'autocar pour _? |
| Is this a direct bus? | ¿Es este un autobús directo? | Ist dies ein direkter Bus? | Est-ce une ligne directe? |
| Which gate does the bus to _____ depart from? | ¿Por cual puerta sale el autobus que va a ____? | Wo fåhrt der Bus nach _____ ab? | Quelle est la porte de départ de l'autocar pour ___? |
| What time does the bus to _____ arrive? | ¿A qué hora llega el autobús que va a a _____? | Wann kommt der Bus nach _____ an? | Quelle est l'heure d'arrivée de l'autocar pour _____? |
| How much is a bus ticket to _____? | ¿Quanto cuesta un boleto de autocar a _? | Was kostet eine Busfahrkarte nach ? | Combien coûte un bille pour _____? |
| Do you accept cash / credit cards / travelers checks for payment? | ¿Acepta usted efectivo/tarjeta de crédito/cheques viajeros para pago? | Kann ich mit Bargeld / Kreditkarte / Reiseschecks bezahlen? | Peut-on payer en espèces/ par carte de crédit/ par travelers check? |
| Do you have any special fare to _____? | ¿Tiene usted alguna tarifa especial para ___? | Gibt es irgendwelche Sondertarife nach _____? | Il y a-t-il des tarifs spéciaux pour _____? |
| Where is the men's restroom? | ¿Dónde están los cuartos de baño para hombres? | Wo ist die Herren-Toilette, bitte? | Où se trouvent les toilettes pour hommes? |
| Where is the women's restroom? | ¿Donde están los cuartos de baño paea mujeres? | Wo ist die Damen-Toilette, bitte? | Où se trouvent les toilettes pour femmes? |
| How many miles is this trip? | ¿Cuántas millas tiene este viaje? | Wie weit ist diese Reise? | Le trajet fait combien de kilomètres? |
| Can you help me find ____? | ¿Me puede usted ayudar a encontrar? | Können Sie mir helfen_ zu finden? | Pouvez-vous me diriger vers _____? |

# TRAVEL NOTES

_____
_____
_____
_____
_____
_____
_____
_____
_____
_____
_____
_____
_____
_____
_____
_____
_____

## IMPORTANT DATES

## THINGS TO BUY

# *ADDRESSES*

Name: _____
Address: _____
_____
Ph:_____ Email: _____

Name: _____
Address: _____
_____
Ph:_____ Email: _____

Name: _____
Address: _____
_____
Ph:_____ Email: _____

Name: _____
Address: _____
_____
Ph:_____ Email: _____

Name: _____
Address: _____
_____
Ph:_____ Email: _____

Name: _____
Address: _____
_____
Ph:_____ Email: _____

Name: _____
Address: _____
_____
Ph:_____ Email: _____

Name: _____
Address: _____
_____
Ph:_____ Email: _____

Name: _____
Address: _____
_____
Ph:_____ Email: _____

Name: _____
Address: _____
_____
Ph:_____ Email: _____

Name: _____
Address: _____
_____
Ph:_____ Email: _____

Name: _____
Address: _____
_____
Ph:_____ Email: _____

## *Important Phone Numbers*

_____
_____
_____
_____

# ▸Useful Info

## ▸Accommodation Symbols Key

| | | | |
|---|---|---|---|
| $ | Money-saving Tip | F | Free Admission/Activity |
| 🏨 | 24 hour reception | 📺 | TV/Common Room |
| ✈ | Free/Cheap Airport Pick-up | 🍴 | Free Breakfast |
| 🚌 | Free/Cheap Bus/Rail Pick-up | 🧳 | Free Linen |
| 📖 | Private Rooms | ☕ | Free Tea & Coffee |
| 💻 | Internet Access | 🌐 | Tour Desk |

## ▸Currency Conversion Chart

| Currency | US$ | € | £ | Yen | C$ | A$ | NZ$ | RAND |
|---|---|---|---|---|---|---|---|---|
| 1 $US | X | €.77 | £.62 | Y82 | $.98 | $.95 | $1.20 | R8.68 |
| 1 € | $1.29 | X | £.81 | Y107 | $1.28 | $1.24 | $1.55 | R11.23 |
| 1 £ | $1.61 | €1.24 | X | Y132 | $1.59 | $1.53 | $1.92 | R13.95 |
| 1 CHF | $1.07 | €.83 | £.67 | Y88 | $1.06 | $1.02 | $1.28 | R9.29 |
| 100 Ft | $.46 | €.35 | £.28 | Y38 | $.45 | $.44 | $.55 | R3.97 |

**Notes:** Column is currencies used during your trip to Europe. Rows are the cost to you in your currency to purchase currencies used in Europe. Ft=Hungarian Forint

## ▸Metric Conversions

**Length**
1 kilometer=0.6 mile
1 mile=1.6 kilometer

**Weight**
1 kilogram=2.2 pounds
1 pound=0.45 kilogram

**Mileage**
30 mph=50 kmh
50 mph=80 kmh
65 mph=105 kmh

**Temperature**
20F=-7C     32F=0C
50F=10C    70F=21C
90F=32C